JOURNEY
BACK TO ME

JOURNEY
BACK TO ME

TOURING THE LANDSCAPE OF MY MIND

SD FERGUSON
ILLUSTRATIONS BY LYNNE HOLTON

BALBOA PRESS
A DIVISION OF HAY HOUSE

Copyright © 2017 SD Ferguson.

All rights reserved. No part of this book may be used or reproduced by any means, graphic, electronic, or mechanical, including photocopying, recording, taping or by any information storage retrieval system without the written permission of the author except in the case of brief quotations embodied in critical articles and reviews.

Balboa Press books may be ordered through booksellers or by contacting:

Balboa Press
A Division of Hay House
1663 Liberty Drive
Bloomington, IN 47403
www.balboapress.com
1 (877) 407-4847

Because of the dynamic nature of the Internet, any web addresses or links contained in this book may have changed since publication and may no longer be valid. The views expressed in this work are solely those of the author and do not necessarily reflect the views of the publisher, and the publisher hereby disclaims any responsibility for them.

The author of this book does not dispense medical advice or prescribe the use of any technique as a form of treatment for physical, emotional, or medical problems without the advice of a physician, either directly or indirectly. The intent of the author is only to offer information of a general nature to help you in your quest for emotional and spiritual well-being. In the event you use any of the information in this book for yourself, which is your constitutional right, the author and the publisher assume no responsibility for your actions.

Any people depicted in stock imagery provided by Thinkstock are models, and such images are being used for illustrative purposes only.
Certain stock imagery © Thinkstock.

Print information available on the last page.

ISBN: 978-1-5043-9057-6 (sc)
ISBN: 978-1-5043-9055-2 (hc)
ISBN: 978-1-5043-9056-9 (e)

Library of Congress Control Number: 2017916628

Balboa Press rev. date: 12/15/2017

For my boys.

We teach what we yearn to master.

We must govern our own lives,
and when our thoughts and actions
become destructive
it is our responsibility to alter or abolish them
and to institute new habits,
as the foundations for
a freer, happier life.

—Brendon Burchard

Table of Contents

1. Asleep at the Wheel 1
2. Gray Thoughts 5
3. In My Head 9
4. Lost in the Past 12
5. Regaining Sight of the Shore 17
6. The What-if Worry Coaster 27
7. In the Now 39
8. The Landscape of My Mind 48
9. Unmerry-Go-Round 54
10. Hills and Holes 56
11. The Fruits We Bear 60
12. The Punishing Room 64
13. Mountain of Lies 67
14. The Bottomless Prayfors 72
15. Knowledge & Knowing 77
16. The Closet of My Mind 82
17. Insults, Injuries & Injustices 86
18. Context Lenses 91
19. Something to Wear 107
20. It's a Practice 115
21. Ready or Not 118
22. Code 1 121

Practice! Catch Yourself! 126
Reading Guide 131
Acknowledgements 133
About the Author 135

Map of My Mind

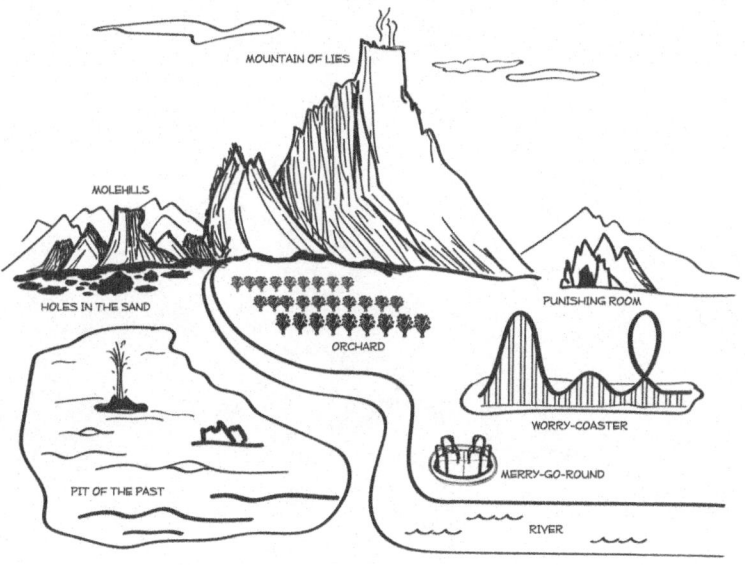

1

Asleep at the Wheel

Today, unlike any day, today, like every other, my thoughts run me. The chatter in my head pulls in one direction while something deep within nudges in another. One voice is vocal and incessant, the other an occasional whisper, one used to calling the shots, the other accustomed to being ignored.

A sharp pain shoots between my temples as I dash to the parking lot, a reminder, I tell myself, of the insanity of back-to-back meetings, each running just enough over to make me late for the next, with too little food and too much caffeine in between. Erica's early morning swim practice, deadlines at work, Jackson's parent-teacher conference, dinner, homework…

Not enough time. Too much to do.

The clicks of my heels on the pavement warn a young mother and her daughter several yards ahead of me of my hurried approach. The mother pulls her daughter close to her, steps back, and yields the sidewalk to me. She fires a glare of disapproval as I go by. "Sorry!" I offer over my shoulder without slowing. "Thank you!"

The sight of my once-again fit body in motion reflected in the deli window sparks a surge of pride and vengeful glee. My overstuffed laptop case swings from one shoulder. My purse sways from the other. The rhythmic flapping of my necklace matches my gait and the bounce of my breasts. Divorce suits me. In the next pane of glass, I detect a jiggle in my reflection where none should be. My smile disappears and takes the spring in my step with it.

I reach the car, toss my bags onto the passenger seat, scan the back seat for the boogeyman, and ignore my growling stomach and ringing phone as I pull out of the parking lot. The clock on the dashboard chides me that it is 3:55. Jackson's school is fifteen minutes away.

The thought of arriving late to my son's parent-teacher conference makes me cringe. I can see it now. My perfectionist ex-husband will glance up at the clock when I enter the classroom. He'll shake his head and roll his eyes in mock disbelief, then let out a sigh as he wraps a protective arm around our son. The teacher, already won over by Michael's charms, will avoid eye contact with me, unwilling to let me off the hook for being late but too cowardly to confront me. And my sweet baby will have that helpless caught-in-the-middle look on his face—the one that breaks my heart.

I try to push the image of my son's conflicted face out of my mind. My imagination resists, running wild instead, fabricating one exaggerated scenario after another, details and outcome slightly altered, each prolonging my self-torment. In one scene I miss the conference altogether. In another, Jackson cries.

Why do I do this to myself?

I honk the horn at an idiot driver who causes me to miss the signal to enter the freeway.

Journey Back to Me

Out the window, billowy white puffs of my favorite kind of cloud hang weightless in the blue sky. Cheerful clusters of pink and white azaleas in full bloom wave to me from the median. I am blind to their splendor. All I want is for the light to turn green.

Minutes later, I cruise down the freeway, lost in thought, my foot too heavy on the accelerator. What will I say to Jackson and his teacher? What excuse is good enough to earn me amnesty?

The ping of a new text message jolts me out of my mental merry-go-round. Without thinking I reach for my phone and read it.

"Need your final price sheet!" the message from my boss reads. In my haste to leave work, I forgot to forward the information my team needs for a sales proposal we have been working on for weeks.

"The deadline for submission is today," it reminds me.

I know I should pull over. But I don't. With my left hand on the steering wheel, I use my right to thumb a reply, glancing from road to phone, phone to road, correcting my path with a jerk whenever my Jeep wanders too close to the dotted lines.

I look up to see the blinking hazard lights of a stalled minivan in my lane. Car to the left of me. Truck on the right. Too fast. Too close. No options.

Panic explodes in my chest.

Tires screech.

I can't bear to look. I've really done it this time.

Fumes of burning rubber reach my nostrils. I hear the crunch of metal against metal. Deep within me, a question awakes from its slumber.

What was I thinking?

2

Gray Thoughts

Silence.

White floods my entire field of vision. My muscles tighten in alarm—each of my senses on full alert. I strain to see something, hear something.

Nothing.

As my eyes acclimate to the brightness, I distinguish movement. All around me wisps of a thick white vapor dance and swirl like the inside of an opaque cloud lit up by the sun.

Where am I? At the same moment the question arises in my head, my own voice, although I have not spoken, thunders above me. "Where am I?" I look up in bewilderment and see a wisp of gray smoke appear and waft amid the white.

"What's that? Am I alive?" my next thoughts boom overhead. Two more gray wisps of smoke join the first to dance in the dazzling white.

"Did I die?" Another gray curl materializes.

"Oh my gosh, I hope I didn't kill someone! Please, no. Anything but that." More wisps, darker than the others.

That's my voice, I think.

"That's *my* voice," echoes at the same instant above me. Another gray wisp is born.

How can that be? I am not speaking!

"How can that be? I am not speaking!" resounds above with the same shakiness in my voice that exists in my head. Two new smoky wisps writhe in the white.

My thoughts? Out loud?

My mind races. Tightness spreads throughout my chest. My breath is shallow, my shoulders tense.

Why are my thoughts out loud and what are those gray swirls? Smoke? Does this mean I am alive? Oh, God. Please, please, don't tell me I'm dead. Or that I hurt someone. I hope I didn't hurt someone!

I hear my thoughts. Am I in a coma?

Panicky thoughts pop in visual gray bursts like monochrome fireworks as the words reverberate above me. Each grim thought seems to generate its own wisp of gray smoke.

"Is this a dream? Am I dreaming?"

Silence.

Gray wisps collide and form bigger wisps.

"Hello? Is anyone out there?" I call out.

No one answers. My fear grows as the acrid smell of smoke stings the back of my throat.

Round and round my mind paces, like a trapped cougar circling its cage to find an escape. Fear fuels my thoughts; my thoughts fuel my fear. *Am I alive? Am I dead? Where am I? How do I get out of here?* I repeat the same unanswered questions in an endless treadmill of thoughts that lead to nowhere.

Smoke overtakes white and I begin to choke. Am I suffocating from my own dark thoughts?

The white is almost gone now.

"I am so afraid!"

I pause, struck by the truth of my admission, unspoken, as it booms through the air. The new gray wisp that accompanies this thought is indistinguishable from the others.

I *am* afraid.

In that moment I know what to do. The silent spawn of a single white wisp goes unnoticed.

As a young girl, my father taught me a technique to calm myself when I was frightened. I narrow my gaze to a single patch of white in the swirling, dancing gray. For a long time, I focus intensely on that little patch of white. Perfectly still, my breathing slows. The coughing stops.

I adjust my listening to ignore the ceaseless chatter of my noisy thoughts being broadcast from above and listen only for my heart. Alas, a faint *tha-thump* in my chest. A delicious feeling of relief expands from my heart outward.

I am alive.

Eyelids closed, I concentrate all my attention on following my breath. In and out.

Slower.

Deeper.

Grounded.

I open my eyes and continue to follow my breath.

Deep inhale.

Slow exhale.

I expand my awareness to include both inside and outside myself, calm.

I adjust my attention to observe my fear-filled thoughts rather than be drawn into them. Maintaining my detachment, I note the cumulative impact the darkness of my thoughts has on my surroundings. Gray. Everywhere.

As I scan the gray, my skin prickles. I freeze. A presence. The thought registers in my mind and chimes above me as I lock eyes with another pair of eyes exactly like my own in the swirling gray.

"There *You* are!" a voice says to me.

Eyes widen.

3

In My Head

My broadcast thoughts and dilated pupils reveal my alarm to my guest.

Am I in danger?

"Trust yourself to know the answer, Liza," the voice says. *"Are you in danger?"*

Eyes anchored on eyes, not daring to move, I take deliberate inventory of my senses in search of an answer. My sense of sight, smell, and hearing are heightened. My body bristles with anticipation, ready to spring. But to my surprise, despite the perceived threat, I do not feel an immediate need to flee. Or fight. Or freeze. Or appease.

My gut tells me I am safe. Safer than I have ever been. My body wilts with relief. Tension carried for years in my neck and shoulders melts. The experience is foreign, exquisite.

With amazement, I answer, "No!" At the exact same time *"No!"* sounds above me, only louder.

"Jinx! You owe yourself a Coke!" the voice says. Eyes twinkle, their outer corners crinkling in amusement. Ah, humor—my preferred method for stress relief. I smile.

"There is rare cause for fear in the moment! The danger is almost always *only* in our head." The eyes glance upward. "In our thoughts."

I follow the eyes upward and ask at the same time my voice above asks, "Where am I?"

"Inside your own head, of course!" answers the voice. "You are *in your mind*!"

"Not *out* of your mind, thank goodness!" the voice chuckles.

"I'm not so sure," I say.

"Would you like the tour?"

"Tour? Tour of what?"

"A tour of the landscape of your mind! Your imagination!"

"Oh. I don't know. Maybe. I mean yes. I think so."

"Aah! Be careful with what you think! There is no telling where your thoughts will take you! It's best to stay here with me!"

"I don't understand. What do you mean, stay here with you? Where could I go?"

"In life, we go where our thoughts take us. Where you focus your attention determines your location. If you are not careful, one thought will lead to another and before you know it, poof! Your imagination will hijack you off to who knows where! So, watch which thoughts you cling to!"

"Wait." I squeeze my eyes shut and shake my head. "I am *in* my *head? In my mind?* With my thoughts?"

"Why, yes."

"But why?" I wonder out loud.

"Isn't that where you spend much of your life? In your head?"

"No!" I answer, just a bit too loud and much too quick. I bite the inside of my cheek, embarrassed at my quick defense of the familiar accusation.

"Well, sometimes," I concede, recalling a past memory, something my daughter once said to me in a heated moment in our kitchen. Was she right? I didn't think so at the time, but now I wonder. I stare at the eyes but I am no longer looking directly into them. My thoughts booming above now sound muffled.

"Stop! Let go of that thought! Don't let it take you away!" shouts the voice.

But it's too late.

"Stay heeeeeeere!"

I hear the voice trail, farther and farther in the distance.

The sensation like that of a warm bubble bath washes over me as the memory of my spat with Erica carries me far away.

I remember it as if was yesterday.

4

Lost in the Past

In an instant, I am standing in the middle of my old kitchen. The last rays of sun settle on the same stubborn wallpaper that took me days to peel off and replace with fresh paint.

The smells of fresh herbs, homemade lasagna, and garlic bread make my stomach growl in anticipation of enjoying Jackson's favorite dinner. Dirty dishes from preparing the meal soak in the old porcelain sink, the suds tainted with pink from the tomato sauce.

The air is tense as my daughter and I complete our ritual of setting the table, with me laying out the plates and napkins and Erica laying out the silverware, refusing to look at me. Each of us is acutely aware of the other's proximity and movements as we circle the table, like two wolves about to fight. The thought of another disagreement with her makes me want to crawl into a hole. With an important work assignment due the next morning, I halfway hope she will continue the silent treatment so I can work all evening in peace.

Erica lays down the final fork, ready for battle. Her stance is defiant and face contorted with anger. The teenage version of myself shrieks at the top of her voice, "Why can't I spend the night with Cheryl? What do you care, Mom? You're not even here when you're here! Your head is *always buried in your laptop or you're doing some project! You wouldn't even notice if Jack and I were dead!"*

"Don't be ridiculous!" I snap.

Her drama irritates me. The fact that her drama reminds me of myself irritates me even more. My voice rises. "You have no clue, Erica! Someone has to make sure you are fed. Someone has to make sure your homework is done! Someone has to work so you..."

Midsentence there is a tiny pop. Incensed with my daughter's ingratitude, I ignore it and continue my rant. Little splatters of dark film from the burst bubble spray through the air. The memory fades. Erica and my house disappear. A sickening odor replaces the delicious aroma of our dinner. And the potent sensation I am floating in a warm bath returns. Along with it comes a flood of regret.

There are so many things I wish I had done differently.

Thick liquid laps gently against me. An unfamiliar hissing sound registers in my ears and snaps me from my reverie. With a clumsy splash, I manage to stand in the water, grateful I can touch the bottom.

What is going on? *Where am I now?* First I was in who-knows-smoky-where. The next minute I am in my old kitchen with my daughter. Now I am here. Where the heck is here?

"You are *in your mind!*" I recall the voice saying. *Did my thoughts take me here?*

I search for the eyes.

The warm bath, it turns out, is a vast steamy pool of murky water filled with thousands of bubbles. Several colorful ones float on the surface near me, their iridescent domes peeking mischievously through the murk, only to submerge back into the gloom a few seconds later. The warmth of the liquid feels silky against my skin, but its pea-green grayish color and a faint whiff of sulfur make me shudder. It is unsettling that I can't see my body just beneath the surface. Not knowing what creatures may lurk beneath, I pull up my feet and begin to tread water in a sludgy circle. Languid ripples travel outward as my arms and legs glide through the murky water and I take in my new surroundings.

Another hiss sounds in the distance. About a mile away, a cannonade of steam rises from an island of dark rocks that jut out of the muck. Seconds later, a massive fountain of water chases the steam, dwarfing the first eruption. Water shoots high in the air and then smashes back down onto the rocks, giving birth to new clouds of steam. Sulfurous vapor drifts toward me, thickening the air. Spellbound, I watch until the surge dies. Thin wisps of white vapor linger like smoke after fireworks. In the peace, beyond the island and geyser, the bright yellow-orange mineral rocks of the shore beckon.

Something ever so light brushes against my leg underneath the dark liquid. Unnerved, I kick my legs and wave my arms to ward off whatever touched me. A sly green bubble rises from the water, grows, and encloses me within it before I have time to resist. Within the bubble, another memory unfolds.

Curled on the couch, I stare at the screen of my laptop, deep in thought. The TV plays a Disney movie the three of us have seen a hundred times, so many I often sing along with the songs without even realizing I am doing so. I am vaguely aware of Jackson as he approaches the arm of the couch with his favorite toy in his hand. I read the email a second time, then click to see who is included on the distribution. My boss and all the other team leads are copied. My stomach lurches. In the background, Jackson whines.

"Mom."

"Just a sec." I read the email again. And again.

"Mom."

"I said just a second."

I hit reply all and craft my response. The force of my fingers as they hit the keys reveals my fury. I review my draft. Needs work. I edit it. Still not happy. I edit again. How could that jerk do this to me? I stop and stare at nothing in particular, motionless, lost in vengeful thoughts.

"But Mommy," Jackson's voice trembles.

"What?" I almost yell, my trance broken.

Jackson burst into tears. "Please, Mommy. It's bwoke." He holds up a piece of his toy in each hand.

I burst into tears. I scoop up my son and hold him close. "It's all right, bud. Mommy's sorry. Let's see if we can fix this."

The bubble bursts, promptly ending the memory. And I stand in the same spot, neck-deep in murky water, heartsick for Jackson, and wishing I could go back.

The bubbles are memories! I touch the nearest bubble, eager to return to my life. Within seconds, a cheerful pink bubble swallows me. Within it, time rewinds. Another memory begins to play.

The air conditioner hums and Ariel's sweet voice sings as I doze. I am slouched in my pajamas, half sitting and half lying on the couch, a cloth diaper draped across my shoulder. Jackson, only eight days old, sleeps on my chest. Erica is sprawled on a blanket palette beside the couch, also fast asleep. Toys and books are strewn all over the floor. The Disney movie is rolling the last credits. I wake from my doze and instinctively take inventory of the whereabouts of my children. What luck! They are both asleep at the same time! It is early afternoon. Having not showered or brushed my teeth, I feel the tug to get up and get something done. I ignore it. Instead, I look down and marvel at the features of my daughter's innocent face and plump little legs. My heart fills with wonder, which grows as my gaze shifts to my tiny son. His dark hair is damp with sweat from the warmth of my body. With each breath, Jackson lifts ever so slightly on my chest and returns closer to my heart with each exhale. Minutes tick by in stillness. I don't dare move. I want this moment to last forever.

There is a small pop. Little bits of pink fall around me.

Back in the hopelessness of the murk, I feel lonelier than I can ever remember. I miss my kids. I want my life back. I want a do-over.

At least I can live through my memories.

Time drifts by, marked by the eruption of the geyser in the distance. I float in my rotten-egg bath reliving my memories and mourn after each comes to an end. Each memory leaves me weak with regret or longing for my loved ones. Yet I yearn for more. Like a junkie, I live only for my next fix.

I can no longer see the shore.

I believe I am lost.

And so I am.

I reach for my next bubble.

5

Regaining Sight of the Shore

A tender memory of when Michael and I were dating ends. I bob in the water, listless, eyes fixed on nothing in particular. Numb.

The eyes!

Visible for only an instant, the eyes vanish behind a cloud of thick vapor from the geyser. With an awkward splash, I lunge in that direction.

"Wait!"

New hope pounds in my chest, only to be dashed as a pale blue bubble covers my elbow, then my shoulder. I try to shake off the bubble and stop its progression.

"No more memories!" I scream. "I want to get out of here!"

The bubble is indifferent to my desires.

Jackson and Erica wave back to me as my ex-husband drives away. I am grateful for the reprieve after a long, exhilarating week. On Monday, my former boss arranged for me to interview with her new company. With no previous experience in software sales, my chance of getting hired seems unlikely. My hopes soar all the same. To get the job would change everything. Even with the child support Michael provides, it is hard to make ends meet. This could be my way out of my financial struggles.

Feeling a little lonely, I walk down to the long row of mailboxes, insert my key into mailbox 232 and twist. The narrow silver door opens to reveal local grocery coupons, a credit card bill, a utility bill, and a distinctive high-quality maize envelope from the software company.

My fingers fumble as I open the envelope, my heart thumping in my chest. I remove a single page of stationery, scan its contents, and let out a victorious yelp of joy when I reach the paragraph that offers me the job. And a substantial increase in salary, too. I hold the letter high in the air and spin in dizzy circles. I did it! I did it!

This time the membrane of the bubble bursts without a sound.

Grinning from ear to ear with my hands still high in the air, I find myself again in the warm bubbly pit of muck. I pull my arms down carefully, wary of nearby bubbles. I turn in a tight deliberate circle on the tips of my toes in hope of spotting the eyes. To my surprise, the shoreline is again visible in the distance. With great care, I navigate toward the rocky island that houses the geyser, skirting any bubbles in my path. My progress is slow.

A dark bubble drifts toward me. I turn sideways to avoid it, and in doing so, I collide with a tiny yellow one. The bubble attaches to my blouse and begins its attempt to enclose me in the past. Rather than stand still, I swim as fast as I can while the unwelcome yellow hitchhiker swells in size. I gain a good distance toward the rocks before the bubble completes its encapsulation and the memory begins.

I am 16. My sister, Gina, is 14. Chrissy is 13. We all clap as Mr. Kumar completes a dance with his bride.

How my sisters and I adore our neighbor, Mr. Kumar! For years we fought over which one of us would get to present him a tray of warm cookies each time we baked them. He would answer the door with glee and devour two or three cookies right in front of us in grand appreciation of our efforts. He had a gift of making each of us feel special. We loved him.

To our dismay, the elderly Mr. Kumar fell madly in love with a creature that did not seem to possess his talents or share his affection for us girls. So, it is with mixed emotions that we now applaud.

The volume and beat of the music increase, the rhythm casting a primitive call to every teenage girl in the pavilion. Meanwhile, the boys, far fewer than girls, make themselves scarce. The dance floor is mostly empty, save for a few older couples Most of us just watch.

My sisters and I ache to dance. We scan the room hopeful to bag a partner but find none, a confirmation that we are condemned to a long evening of watching the festivities from the sideline. We make no attempt to hide our annoyance when my mother suggests that we should dance with each other. Instead, we sulk, each of us irritated with everyone else.

A song we all recognize from my parents' youth begins to play. To our surprise, my father takes my mother's hand and leads her to the dance floor. Their synchronized movements are fluid and graceful. I swell with pride. My father sings to my mother. The music is too loud to distinguish his voice, but the serenade is unmistakable. He holds her close, one hand caressing the small of her back. The years melt away as we watch my middle-aged parents transform to two young people in love. I am mesmerized. I look over at Chrissy and Gina and they look over at me. With a glance, the sacred connection and bond only sisters share are strengthened, forged with the awe this extraordinary glimpse of life endows.

Mr. Kumar approaches us, arms open wide, a huge grin on his face.

"My girls! My beautiful girls! We dance!"

As much as I want to dance, I dread the prospect of the crowd learning how poorly I do so. The dance floor is empty. I will be exposed.

But, there is no time to protest. The exchange of anxious looks between my sisters assures me I am not alone in my fear. Unwilling to disappoint our elated friend we join Mr. Kumar on the dance floor. The four of us make a small circle and dance. Mr. Kumar does a twitchy jig that makes us all laugh. Our reserved biologist is not going to let unfamiliarity with dance ruin his celebration! His freedom to be his self boosts our confidence. I set aside my fear of what others may think.

I let go.

My sisters sense the shift and follow. We dance, carefree. Mr. Kumar beams. Our fun is infectious and spreads to include my mother and father. We dance more. We laugh. The new Mrs. Kumar joins us, all smiles. We join hands and swing to the music. Joyous. We take turns dancing in the center. We laugh and cheer. Our circle grows bigger. We twirl and circle and twist and shout.

We are silly.

We are happy.

We are alive.

I buzz with the celebration of this moment and the depth of my love for these people with whom I dance. My beautiful mom. My dad. Gina, Chrissy, Mr. Kumar, and yes, his misjudged bride.

A loud pop sounds.

The music stops. I hear the geyser erupt and sigh in recognition of my return. Such a magical evening! I had almost forgotten about Mr. Kumar. It was so long ago! The memory reminds me that there is so much freedom when you stop caring about what others think and just focus on the people and things you love. Why don't I remember that more often?

Journey Back to Me

I note my distance from the island. Good! I moved at least 300 yards closer.

Is it possible to continue swimming while I relive the memory? Deliberately, I reach out and touch a small gray bubble, then duck under the liquid and push against the bottom to propel my body forward. I surface with my head down, feet kicking and arms moving in a well-practiced crawl. The action slows the encapsulation process. When the bubble completes its enclosure around me, I continue my crawl inside the bubble. My progress is slower, but the overall result is favorable. The bubble buoys in the general direction of the rocks.

I hope this will be a good memory.

I am in fifth grade. I stay a few minutes after school to ask my teacher a question about the science homework. Afterwards, I hurry to catch up with my friends so we can walk the rest of the way home together. Seeing them ahead, I quicken my pace. As I get closer, I overhear Betsy and Claire's conversation.

"She thinks she's so smart," says Claire, in the biting gossipy tone all fifth-grade girls have mastered.

"But she's not," says Betsy with the authoritative air of the most popular girl at school. "I can't believe she wore that stupid shirt again."

Both girls giggle.

I freeze on the sidewalk, fearful of discovery. I feel sucker-punched. I know I am the one who thinks she's so smart. And I am the one who is wearing that stupid shirt again, my favorite shirt, the one I will never wear again.

The bubble bursts.

I brusquely brush off the little bits of gray bubble that land on me, quick to be rid of a memory that was instrumental in shaping my trust in others and a reassessment of myself. The sting of betrayal is just as fresh as the first day it happened.

I look back to measure my progress. Not so great. Why?

My energy plummets. Annoyed, I slap a pretty gold bubble as it surfaces, callous to the beauty of its shiny surface as it glints in the sun. I go under, push myself from the bottom and race toward the rocks as the languid gold bubble covers me in its ball gown-colored enclosure. "Great. All I need is some glass slippers," I mutter before I slip into the memory.

I am 28. The sun shines brightly through the living room window, nature's attempt to mask the frigid weather outside. Snuggled under a lap quilt, I alternate between inhaling the aromatic steam and taking small sips of my peppermint tea as I read my book. A fresh idea pops into my mind. My eyebrows lift in surprise and I snap my book closed, not bothering to mark the spot I stopped reading. A tingling sensation travels up my forearms in celebration of an epiphany. I finally see how the barriers that have prevented me from starting my own business can be overcome! Success is within reach if I strive for it.

Gears turn inside my skeptical head. I explore the pros and cons, weigh the risks and probability of success. I conduct a mental inventory of resources and am satisfied. I must be sure. Outward, I am peaceful, serene. Inside, I soar from the resurrection of a dream that I long concluded as dead and is now alive.

I know exactly what I need and what to do. I gulp down my cold tea and run to get my laptop.

While I swim, the golden bubble suffers a leak, then deflates and collapses, leaving behind an oily golden residue that sticks to my skin. I continue my forward stroke. Other bubbles brush against me but slide away, unable to stick, because my skin still glistens with the golden residue from the last bubble.

Passion rekindled from the memory sustains the momentum of my swim. Swirling with possibility, my mind races. I swim to catch up with it. I push away thoughts of past failures and ignore the fact that I eventually pronounced the pursuit of dreams to be quixotic. Instead, I revel once again in the euphoria that clarity in purpose provides. The island gets closer. My conviction grows stronger. I swear if I get a second chance I won't let anything get in my way again.

When my arms and legs tire, I take a small break, then resume my crawl, determined to reach the island. A bubble the size of a basketball emerges from the murk, rolls up my back, and encloses around me in one fluid motion while I swim.

He shakes his head no. His words are apologetic and kind.

But.

But.

How can he say no? I gave this so much thought!

"I would love to Liza. It's a great idea, but I just can't. Not right now. I'm sorry."

No.

No!

This can't be. He is the perfect partner to help me with my new business. He is bright. Our strengths are complementary. I trust and respect him. He trusts and respects me.

At least I thought so.

Hurt and humiliation rise hot in my cheeks. I open my eyes wide and blink to calm the sting, unable to hear the validity of his explanation.

"Until we know Sarah is ok, which could take a couple of years, I can't even think about changing our medical coverage. It could be disastrous for us."

"Of course, not! What was I thinking?"

I backpedal and make a wisecrack. The false cheer in my laugh, just a little too loud, sounds like nails on a chalkboard. He changes the subject.

A seed of doubt takes root. I was so sure of myself. Why didn't I see this coming?

Where else did I miscalculate?

I sit across the desk from my friend, legs crossed, dressed in a new outfit I bought for the occasion. The emerald silk blouse is now ruined from nervous sweat and I hate myself for buying it.

What a fool I am.

I nod politely as he tells a story. I do my best to pretend to listen. But I can't. All I want to do is run and hide.

The memory ends. I spin around in the water. How can this be? I am farther from the island, not closer. Was I swimming the wrong way? Is it possible my state of mind influences my results? I reject the thought, still agitated from the memory.

I still can't believe he said no. I think to myself.

He didn't say no. He said he couldn't, I argue.

What's the difference? If I can't persuade my best friend, I can't persuade anybody. Might as well give up.

Giving up was the worst mistake of my life.

Yeah, but who else can I trust? Nobody!

While the argument in my head rages I hit my knee hard on a massive volcanic rock hidden beneath the surface. "Oww!" With my hand, I feel for the offending obstacle, find it, and lean against it to examine my wound.

The conflict continues.

I can still find someone! You don't give up on your dreams. You just don't!

Yeah, but nothing has changed. I'll probably just fail again.

Distracted by the stormy discord within myself, I lose both my footing and the struggle to keep my balance. My left foot slips into a crevice between two large rocks. I howl with pain.

No matter how I twist and turn my foot, I cannot free my ankle from between the rocks. I take a deep breath and duck my head under the water to try to pull my ankle free. I come up sputtering, take another deep breath and submerge again. This time I push against the rocks in an attempt to increase the width of the crevice that holds my ankle tight. I fail.

I am stuck.

My dark clouds of doubt fill the sky. The wind starts to blow. The waters grow choppy. It is difficult for me to keep the muck out of my mouth and nose. The storm in my head competes with the storm in the sky. I yank at my foot some more. But neither the rocks nor my bleeding ankle budge.

Oh, no! Not good!

What if I drown?

What if I can't get free?

What if...? The question provides all the encouragement my imagination needs to go wild. Gagging on a mouthful of muck, I conjure the first exaggerated image of what could possibly happen as my worries take me for a ride.

Thunder rumbles. A bright flash of lightning cracks through the sky, illuminating the rocks and the fact I am no longer there.

6

The What-if Worry Coaster

"Ouch!" I yell, still spitting and gagging from the muck I swallowed.

I lean over to see what the heck is stabbing the back of my knee. There is just enough light to identify the villain responsible for my pain. The jagged end of an upholstery welt protrudes from the split seam of the worn seat cushion on which I sit. I scoot over a couple of inches to avoid it.

Where did my thoughts take me this time?

I sit back up and notice two big signs to my left. Each is lit with a single bare bulb. The first sign has a large red arrow. In dark block letters, it reads, "DECISIONS MADE THIS WAY."

The second sign shows a yellow yardstick with an arrow that points to 26 inches. "YOU MUST BE TALLER THAN 26" AND AT LEAST 8 MONTHS OLD TO RIDE." *What?*

The car lurches forward and I grab the seat to keep from toppling backward. I sit in the first and only car of an old roller coaster. And it is moving. I grab the door and open it, ready to jump.

I look down.

Maybe not.

Nothing but black. A bottomless black.

The speed of the car increases. I close the door, alarmed to see the top hinge is damaged.

Another sign goes by.

NO EXIT

"NO EXIT."

The clickety-clack gets louder as the speed of the car accelerates. A voice, *my voice*, crackles over the loudspeaker, "There is no exit. For your safety, please remain in the car with your seat belt fastened until we come to a full and complete stop at the unloading point of the ride. If the ride stops temporarily due to mechanical failure or other reasons, stay seated and wait for the ride to start up again or for an operator to give you further instructions. Do not, I repeat, do not exit the car. Thank you."

The car jerks, causing me to lose my balance and fall onto the bench. The exposed upholstery welt jabs me again. I let out a yelp, scoot over a few inches, and scramble to find my seat belt.

The filthy polyester webbing that once formed the two joining pieces of a seatbelt dangle from corroded bolts on each side of the car. The seat belt insert on the right is intact but the buckle needed for the left side is missing—cut clean by something very sharp. I throw down the end of the cut belt and reach above me to grab the safety bar. I pull down and hold my breath, praying it, too, is not broken. The safety bar mechanism locks into place.

A few seconds later, the car approaches an ornate arched entrance lit with huge letters that spell out, "WHAT IF?" As the car passes under the arch, all lights sniff out. The car jerks to a half-second halt and then starts up a steep incline. My heart thumps like a drum in my chest. Fear rises in my throat.

I hate roller coasters.

I grip the safety bar tight and strain to see in the dark. The car goes up, and up, and up. The pulley and cable groan with the weight of the car as if it weighs a thousand pounds. Every few seconds, the cable slips, then catches again with a jerk, sending me into a frenzy of terror. As the car makes its ascent, I know without question, something bad is going to happen.

Something very bad.

Outside to the left of the car I am shocked to see an image of myself standing in the parking lot below. It looks like I am waiting for someone. A dark figure appears behind me and stands so close I can feel his warm breath on my neck. I lock eyes with the me in the parking lot. I know I am in trouble. I can see the terror shine in my own eyes.

Out of the right side of the car, another scene unfolds. I watch myself grab the keys off the kitchen counter on my way to the garage. I open the Jeep door and throw my purse on the passenger seat. The garage door I forgot to close is already open. I start to back out of the driveway. Looking in the rearview mirror, I first check the backseat for the boogeyman—an absurd habit I started in high school after

Gina and I watched our first, and my last, horror film about a serial killer who hid in the back seats of his victims' cars. Michael used to love to tease me about it.

At the same moment, both of us, the me on the roller coaster and the me inside the Jeep, catch sight of a shock of red hair peeking out from under a blanket used days earlier for a picnic. Just like the movie! There is someone hiding in the back seat of the Jeep!

Both of us freeze, not knowing what to do, transfixed by the uncovered tuft of greasy hair.

The roller coaster pully strains and protests. The car slips, catches, and climbs higher.

Further to the right, I see another me, sound asleep in my own bed. I awaken. In the darkness, I sense something is wrong. There is someone in the house. There is someone in my room. Next to the bed. He stands over me, knife held high.

The car jerks to a stop as it reaches the top, then teeters on the edge of the precipice for an eternal moment of absolute silence. The intruder raises his knife higher. The roller coaster car plummets. Both of us scream. The knife goes in. I clutch onto the bar as my butt lifts off the seat. My stomach reaches my throat as the car screams down the rails. I scream too. Blood rushes to my head.

On the way down, I witness the red-haired stranger under the blanket pop up in the back seat. He twists a wire around my neck. The man in the parking lot grabs me from behind as the car careens to the right and then jerks violently to the left on its ever-downward path. With every twist and turn, I witness myself harmed.

The car rounds a sharp curve. The inertia pulls me to the side door. It opens. I use all my strength to keep from being flung out of the car. The car rounds another curve in the opposite direction. The door slams shut. I am hurled to the other side. Outside the car, I see Michael reading a book at a picnic table. Erica and Jackson run along a ledge where a river runs several feet below. Jackson tosses a stick into the current and runs alongside to follow its path downstream.

My children round a bend, no longer in Michael's sight. He never watches the kids as close as he should.

My heartbeat quickens.

Erica pleads with Jackson to be careful. With his eye on the stick, Jackson trips over a rock running at full speed. He topples over the edge into the current. His head and body disappear under the water and reappear several yards ahead. Arms and legs flail only to submerge again. I hold on as the car dips and turns, grimacing with each bump and swerve, but I do not take my eye off the current.

Erica runs along the edge. Her screams to Jackson echo in my ears. In desperation, Erica jumps into the water.

"Nooooooooooooooo!" I scream.

Both bodies wash up on the shore, face down.

The car dips again and begins its descent down in a corkscrew spiral. I see Erica drown in a swimming pool. Michael chokes to death in the school lunchroom. Then Erica reappears in a hospital bed surrounded by doctors who are clueless how to treat her unknown disease.

As the car nears another curve, I see Erica leave the house in an unfamiliar skirt that is way too short. She should be in school. Erica skips down the sidewalk, her dark hair flowing in the breeze. She is so lovely. A lump rises in my throat. I clutch the safety rail even tighter. I close my eyes to hold the beauty of my daughter's innocence in my memory as long as I can.

All the while a feeling of more pending tragedy builds within me.

A sparkling white convertible pulls up with three other teens. I recognize one of the girls—Cheryl—a friend of Erica's whom I never trusted. Music blares. Erica jumps in. The convertible speeds off. The wind carries the music and their laughter to my ears. The pretty blonde in the back seat takes a long swig from a bottle and passes it to the driver.

I feel queasy.

I already know the outcome.

The roller coaster car picks up speed as it goes round and round in a spin. I vomit.

The convertible full of teenagers swerves to avoid a tree, then collides with a truck traveling in the opposite direction.

"Noooooooooo!" I scream again.

I squeeze my eyes closed as the car slows and ascends a slight incline. The ride evens out for a stretch. I open my eyes and relax my grip on the safety bar. The smell of my own sweat and vomit permeates the air. The carnage of my worst fears is on full display.

Click. Click. Click.

Gears grind.

The pulley begins its protest again and the car begins a second ascent. Numb, I look away as the distance between the horrors on the ground and the rising car in which I sit lengthens.

I slump in my seat, my adrenaline depleted, incapable of a coherent thought. The only thing I am aware of is how much my knuckles ache from gripping the safety bar. I open and close my fists several times to uncramp the muscles and ease the pain. I no longer have the will or energy to inch away from the wretched upholstery welt that jabs the tender back of my knee.

More than halfway up the incline, I still do not notice the seismic sea wave barreling down on the rickety roller coaster. The wall of water looms larger and closer.

I sense the wall of water before I see it. The unease starts in my gut.

The wave is huge. How did I miss it? I have to look up to see the top of the wave. My gaze follows the wave back down where the water is gobbling up everything in its path.

A tsunami? That's impossible.

Journey Back to Me

My brain tries to catch up to what my intuition already knows. Everything I care about will soon be destroyed.

I smell the seawater and take a huge gulp of air.

I have never been good at holding my breath. What do I have, two minutes? Max? I accept my fate. Remnants of the community I lived in since birth float by me in slow motion like a silent movie. I recognize the clock from the library, a brown UPS truck, a guitar, and shoes, tons of shoes, probably from the Payless on Fifth Street.

Twenty yards away, several drowned corpses haunt the waters.

I look away.

The car bumps into a large box. The soggy cardboard seams give way. Hundreds of music CDs packaged in jewel cases break free. They swirl like confetti all around me.

I am out of air.

The water darkens as the entire pylon sign from the sports arena floats above me and blocks the sun.

To my astonishment, the coaster continues.

Water gushes out of the car on both sides. The damaged top door hinge gives way even further to allow the water to escape. Ahead is a series of hills, rapid ups and downs followed by a wide turn. I think I'm going to be sick again.

Up, up, up.

I brace myself for the fall. On the way down, bombs fall on my hometown. Buildings are reduced to ash and piles of cement covered rebar. On the second hill, I lose everything in a tornado, then a flood, hurricane, and fire. I lean into the next deep curve filled with dread of what could possibly be next.

It is a flat stretch.

I let go of the safety bar and relax, exhausted. Ahead is an even steeper climb. I scoot over to lie on the bench as the car rocks slowly upward. I close my eyes and curl my arms around the safety bar. The grinds and groans of the machinery lull me into a fitful doze.

Higher and higher.

What if?

What if?

Two women laugh. Their laughter carries across the dark. It is an unkind laugh, certain to be at another's expense. "Did you see the look on her face?" says one of the women. Both women laugh again, louder than before. "I know! I know! I would die of embarrassment if that was me!" says the other, setting off another peal of laughter. A pained look crosses my face as I rest. I draw my head, arms, and legs closer to my torso as if to hide.

The car begins its descent. Outside the car and inside my dreams, people in my life appear in one incident after another. Each results in increased feelings of embarrassment, humiliation, betrayal, and shame for me.

I am slandered.

I am judged.

I try to block out the images and voices. But there is no escape, no exit, just as the signed warned. Outside the car or inside my head, asleep or awake, eyes opened or closed, my humiliation progresses without so much as a pause. Hidden secrets revealed, modesty violated, and trust in myself and others is shattered and destroyed.

Both the roller coaster car and my sense of self-worth nosedive.

I plunge into despair.

The car takes a sharp turn and quick dip that snaps me back into survival mode. Another version of myself comes into view outside the car. This me is studying her reflection in the mirror, searching for a new wrinkle, a blemish, or any stray unwelcome hair. I spy a small growth on my cheek. It begins to grow in size until my face is disfigured.

On the opposite side of the car, another version of myself steps into the shower. With a hand full of shower gel I begin to lather my body. Steam rises. I close my eyes in peace. As I rinse the suds off my breasts, my fingers run over what feels like a lump. My eyes shoot open. I feel the spot again.

It's a big lump.

I panic only to discover an even larger one in my armpit.

My disease progresses. I watch as I suffer from the helplessness and hopelessness of the incurable. I see myself bedridden, only able to eat through a tube. I need assistance to use the restroom.

The loss of dignity is too much for me to bear. A loud groan escapes my lips.

Next, I witness the progressive ruin of my adult body through the hateful process of aging. My cherished dark, luxurious hair, once the envy of women everywhere, is now sparse, gray, wiry, and lusterless. The allure of my full breasts and hips is gone. I am alone, never remarried.

Old.

Alone.

No one to love.

No one to love me.

I squeeze my eyes closed.

What more can fear conjure?

The car takes a quick turn and scales an incline. The increased height and propulsion of the turn cause the car to gain speed again on its way down, down, down into an iterative nightmare.

Ding! I look out of the car and see another me. I watch myself glance at my cell phone to read an alert from my bank. My account is overdrawn. How can that be?

Ding!

My life savings is gone.

Ding! Ding!

I am destitute, not a penny to my name.

A set of spirals spurs familiar recurring fears. What if? What if?

The economy goes into a recession. I stay in a job I despise.

The economy goes into a depression. I lose my job and am unable to find another.

The stock market crashes. My 401k funds evaporate overnight.

I start my own business and fail.

And fail.

And fail.

A few seconds later the ride ends its spiral.

Anger.

Grief.

Helplessness.

Humiliation.

I am exhausted from my mind's ruin of everything I care about. My life, the safety of my family, my financial security, community, country, and reputation. All the people, places, and things I love.

"Stop! Whoever you are, please stop! I want off!" I beg.

There is no answer.

The roller coaster car reaches the bottom of the hill and coasts on level ground. No more spins. No more spirals. Thank God.

Why am I here?
Who is doing this to me?

"No!"

Oh, yes. I freeze as the answer to my question surges through my body. Could I be doing this to myself? Everything I just witnessed has one thing in common. The horrors are familiar. *I* am their author. Entertained only once or a thousand times, rational or absurd, these are *my* fears, *my* worries. My *thoughts*.

The car slows and enters a poorly lit tunnel.

To my left, a sign passes. It reads, "IT COULD HAPPEN!"

A second sign reads in large red letters: "THINK." Underneath in smaller black letters, it asks, "WHAT ARE YOU GOING TO DO?"

Ahead I see a huge ornate arch that matches the one at the entrance of the ride. It is lit with large letters that read: "DECISION POINT." The car crawls as it approaches the arch and then comes to a complete stop. To my right, I see the exit. To my left, not far from the car, another version of myself is slumped against the wall, her arms wrapped around her knees, rocking back and forth in terror. A sinister beast creeps toward her with a low growl. I look away.

The sound of my own voice over a loud speaker makes me jump "Please look around you and check under your seat. Take all your belongings and worries with you and exit to your right. Thank you for riding the What-if Worry Coaster." A buzz sounds and the safety bar rises. With a creak, the car door opens. The top hinge crumbles.

The door drops with a loud scraping noise and dangles from the car, held only by the bottom hinge.

I remain seated, pondering the words on the arch.

Decision Point.

The absurdity of it all sinks in. How many times have I put myself on this emotional roller coaster? How much time have I wasted worrying about every possible thing that could go wrong in my life, what could happen or what others may think or do or say? How many poor decisions have I made based on unrealistic fears? Hundreds.

No.

Thousands.

And how many actually happened?

Outside the car, the other me is still rocking in fear. The menacing beast crouches, ready to pounce, fangs bared. Instinctively I shrink back only to be jabbed one last time by the bastard upholstery welt.

Enough! I reach underneath me to grab the welt and give it a fierce jerk to free it from the cushion. Victorious, I hold the welt up and scoot all the way to the left side of the car. I take one last look into the eyes of the frightened me huddled outside the car. With my heart thumping hard and teeth clenched, I stretch my arm out as far as I can and touch the snarling beast with the ridiculous plastic welt.

Pleh!

She disappears. The beast disappears.

My laughter echoes through the tunnel. Loud. Jubilant. Victorious.

What if?

What a fool I have been! My fears and worries are not real. They never were. They exist only in my head.

The truth frees me.

7

In the Now

In an instant, I am back in the thick white fog. The warm pair of eyes exactly like my own blinks an acknowledgement of my return.

"Welcome back! I see you started the tour of your mind without me!"

The tension that racks my body eases in the presence of the now familiar eyes and voice. Even the swirling white feels reassuring.

"Lost in the mind can be a terrible place to be! Now, we don't want your thoughts wandering off with you again," the voice chuckles, eyes crinkling in the corners. In a serious tone, the voice says "Liza," and then pauses. I turn to meet the eyes, my full attention on them.

"Remember what I said. Here in the mind, just as in life, you go where your thoughts take you. Where you focus your attention determines your location. You are either here in the Now or in one of four other places."

I nod.

"Lost in the past. You've been there."

Yes.

"Captive in your imagined future."

"Done that," my thoughts say above. "The worry coaster," I say aloud.

"Absorbed in thought," the voice continues. "Or, you're in the punishing room."

I don't like the sound of the last of the four places. I dare not ask what it is. My thoughts might take me there.

"When your focus is here, now, you will remain with me. We will be free to explore. However, if your attention drifts to other things, you will find yourself *elsewhere* in the mind."

"So how do I stay with you?"

"You focus your attention on what is in front of you and around you, here, and now. To do this, you must distance yourself from your thoughts. You see, thoughts are things with great power."

Stay in the now? Focus on what's in front of me? I listen with intent. I have no interest in returning to the swamp of memories or the roller coaster. Both my thoughts and the jittery rolls my stomach turns express my concerns. "I don't know how to stay in the Now."

"It is not something most of us are accustomed to doing. It takes discipline to keep your focus, here, in the Now. Yet, that's the only place life happens—in the Now! Never in the mind! Look neither ahead nor backward. The past is gone! And the future is only imagined! There is truly only *Now*!"

I hang on to the word *life* as soon as it is spoken, not hearing anything said afterward. "Life?" echoes above me. I force my attention back to the conversation and pretend my thoughts did not try to wander.

"Perfect demonstration! Did you notice that?" asks the voice, eyes looking upward. "When I said, 'Life only happens here and now,' for a moment your focus was drawn to the word *life*. If you continued to cling to that thought, instead of listening to what was being said, that thought would have carried you away."

"I felt it! I had to fight to pull my attention back. But, it really wanted to go there."

"Yes!" says the voice. "When your awareness shifts to zero in on something, that split-second fixation creates a tremendous pull for your exclusive attention. Once you engage with a thought, you are stuck. It is difficult to rid yourself of it. Like chewing gum on the bottom of your shoe!"

I smile.

"Notice the pull. When you feel it, resist the temptation to follow it and just stay here with me. Your broadcast thoughts are your warning system. When they sound, redirect your attention to what is in front of you Now."

"But, I feel the pull now. Right now. Life! My life? I want to know! Will I ever go back to my life?"

"Notice how much energy you expend looking outside yourself to gain peace. The peace you seek is available if you look inward, never outward. Look for yourself, dear Liza. Trust yourself."

Despite the encouragement, I resist. I don't want to look for myself or trust myself. I just want the answer. No, I just want the answer I want. I hear my thoughts and cringe. I sound like a three-year-old when she does not get her way.

"More energy," reports the voice gently.

I feel the drain. My thoughts reveal my inner churn.

Silence.

I squirm and then, at last, blurt, "I am afraid the answer inside will be the one I don't want. That I'll never go back."

"Yes. And that may be. An unexamined fear can be very powerful. It increases its potency through repetition of the thought and our avoidance of the emotions it brings with it. We hope it will go away. It does not," says the voice.

"Hope is never a good strategy," I say, one of my favorite expressions.

"By avoiding the fear, the thought occupies more and more space in your mind."

I am quiet again.

"How will you ever know if you run from the fear and never question its validity?"

"I won't," I concede.

I am still, then sigh long and deep.

My jaw and shoulders relax as the internal struggle dissipates. I look inward and inquire. After several minutes, I see there is not an answer. It cannot be discovered or given. Nor is the answer withheld from me. I do not know if I will return home. The answer *is* something other than what I wanted. But not knowing is better than the "I'll never go back" I presumed. I stop resisting not knowing. I am at peace with the truth of it.

Within a few seconds, another fearful thought rushes to replace the one dispelled moments earlier. The tension in my jaw and shoulders returns.

"When one fear releases its grip, often another springs forward to take its place. Remember, thoughts are just things. Your fear of no return is just a thought, Liza. All there is right here and Now is you, me, and your fearful thought to keep you company. Examine the thought as an outsider. Distance yourself from it."

"How do I distance myself from my thoughts? Aren't they part of me?"

"No. You are not your thoughts and your thoughts are not you. They are only the you that you think you are and forgot you are not. Let me show you. Remember your father's trick, the one where you pick a focal point, concentrate on it, and block everything out to calm your mind?"

I nod my head.

"Instead of picking a small spot, we will pick a big one: everything around us. And instead of blocking everything out, we focus initially on just our breathing and then expand our attention to observe everything. We do nothing and watch everything, outside and inside. We listen. We notice. But we do not act or respond. We look. We listen, We breathe. Learn to play the role of observer, with no attachment whatsoever to what is going on or what thoughts appear. We will thought-watch, not thought-cling. Are you ready?"

"I think so." But my thoughts, going off like fireworks above, disagree.

I rub my sweaty palms together and shake my head at the beehive of thoughts that sound above me.

"Relax," says the voice. "Just breathe. When there is a buildup of nervousness, fear, or strong desire inside, our thoughts become extremely active. We'll walk through it together."

My gratitude, expressed when our eyes meet, is accepted and acknowledged with a slow blink. "Deep breath in, Liza. Deep breath out. Just breathe. In and out. Now bring your awareness to your body. Feel its sensations. And keep breathing. Now expand your awareness to include your surroundings. Just stay aware of what is occurring now and let's eavesdrop on your thoughts. Let the thought rise and be heard and then let the thought go."

I am still. I feel my chest rise and fall. I am aware of the white fog swirling about me and the kind eyes looking into my own. I feel the soothing quality of the voice and hear my own thoughts heralded above me.

"Easy. Easy. Don't think. Just breathe," booms above. "Those eyes look so familiar. Concentrate! How can I concentrate when all I can hear is my thoughts? They never shut up. Do they? Is that what this is all about? Shhhhh! I don't think I am doing this right. My ankle still hurts. How can my ankle hurt if I am dead? I must be alive. I want to go home to my kids and my life. Stop. Let it go. Let the thought go."

Seconds go by in silence. My thoughts start up again. "Four places I can go? I hope the other places are not like the roller coaster. Let it go. Breathe. Stay in the now. What is the punishing room? Let it go, Liza. Let it go. Am I here in the now? I don't even know what that means!"

My energy fluctuates as I tense and relax in response to my thoughts. I notice the strength of the pull some thoughts possess over others.

After a bit, I realize if I loosen my shoulders, it is easier to focus. I can feel the space between myself and my thoughts expand. I hear the thoughts as clearly as before but the pull for my attention is muted. My whole body no longer reacts or responds to them. The contrast is noticeable and welcome. I am calmer.

Moments later, my shoulders are tense again but I have no clue when or how I tightened them. My impatience builds.

"This is hard! How can I be tense again?" My thoughts spin on another cycle of random musings. Some thoughts seem connected; others seem to come out of nowhere. Only minutes have passed, but I am ready for the exercise to be over. I fidget and shift the weight of my body, then shrug my shoulders to release the tension. "How much longer?" resounds above.

"Ok," the voice interrupts after a few seconds of silence. I am relieved it is over.

"Did you notice your thoughts?"

"Yes. Kind of embarrassing. I sound like a lunatic."

We both laugh.

"So, if that is you doing all the thinking, who is it that watches and listens as your thoughts appear?"

The back of my neck prickles. I feel an empty space between my ears—that peacefulness I experienced as I observed my thoughts. And I feel my...my... *what is it?* I feel some part of myself struggle with the question. I don't see it. I grasp and search into the empty space in my head for the answer. I find nothing. My thoughts go wild above my head. "Who is it? What is watching the thoughts? Who is thinking the thoughts?"

Whatever or whoever it is, it is gone.

"Did I chase it away?"

"Liza."

Our eyes meet. "Trust yourself. Who is watching the thoughts? Be still and look inside for the answer." The expanse in my head is now gone, crowded by my excited thoughts. I pay the thoughts no heed and focus on stilling myself again.

After several minutes, the expanse of peacefulness shifts to my chest. I become aware. I hear and observe my thoughts and watch myself observe and hear my thoughts. The distinction of the part of me that thinks the thoughts and the part of me that observes them comes into focus.

Who is watching?

I don't have words.

I peer further.

It is a knowing, a presence, some kind of intelligence that does not speak but in the silence communicates as clear as a bell.

"My soul?" I ask, unsure of what to call the wondrous being that dwells within.

"That is the real You. You are not the lunatic who also resides in your head. That gal is the you that you think you are when you forget it isn't you."

"Oh," I say. "When I am my thoughts, the real me doesn't show up. When I watch my thoughts, I do!"

"Yes! The real You goes away when your attention goes myopic. And that is how You stay here with me—by being aware of your thoughts, instead of hijacked by them," says the voice.

"But all I can think about is going home. I made so many mistakes. I want to go back."

"How would you live your life differently, Liza? Be careful. Stay here with me in the present when you answer so you don't end up reliving your regrets in the Pit of the Past."

A lump in my throat makes it hard for me to swallow. My voice breaks as I answer, "I would…" I stop to get my emotions under control.

The eyes are soft.

"Sorry."

I brush away tears and try again. "I would live more. I would show my love more. It sounds so trite, so cliché. There was so much I could have and wanted to do. But I held back. I don't even know what I was so afraid of."

"Do you want to know?"

"Yes. I do."

The eyes smile.

The white fog rolls away like curtains drawn back on a stage and disappears within seconds. The sun shines brightly on the wondrous landscape that is my mind.

"Nothing like clarity to make the fog of confusion disappear!" the voice shouts.

8

The Landscape of My Mind

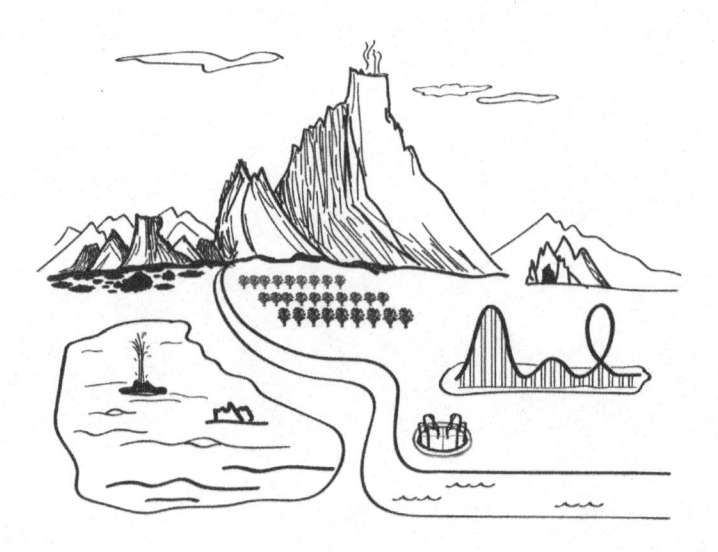

I inhale a deep breath and soak it all in. An anemic river winds through the land, its high banks and large dry riverbeds an indication of its previous size and power. On the horizon, to my far left, are clusters of innumerable small mountains that form a long range that extends as far as I can see. In front of the mountain range, there is a large volcanic mud pool and geyser. On the other side of the river, farthest away, is a huge volcano with forests at its base and an orchard-filled valley. To the far right, I see more hills, what looks like a cave, and a monstrous roller coaster. I shudder.

"Now, where were we?" asks the voice. "Ah, yes! Fear! We have the best seats in the house! Almost everything we see is shaped by your fears, starting before you were even a year old. It is your habitual thoughts and emotions that create the landscape of your mind."

"I see the worry coaster over there!"

"Yes, the ride of needless dread for what tomorrow may bring! Whenever we are fearful of what may happen in the future, our thoughts take us on a grand roller coaster ride. We experience every imaginable horror again and again in our thoughts, unable to stop them."

"I used to ride some version of that thing every day," I admit. "And many nights," I add. "It's exhausting."

"Funny, most often reality doesn't remotely match what we imagine, yet when we make decisions we give our fears disproportional consideration."

"Yes, I can see that *now*."

"Even the smallest of worries can consume tremendous amounts of time, energy, and attention."

"If I let them," I say.

"Yes," says the voice. "*Only* if you let them."

Remembering the confusing sign, I ask, "Why did the sign say you must be at least eight months old to ride?"

"As early as eight months of age, we begin to show evidence of fearing the future. A baby shows anxiety when its mother is no longer in sight or if she thinks her mother is going to leave her."

"Separation anxiety?"

"Yes," says the voice. "The beginning of concern for what could happen."

"Is that the swamp of memories over there?" I ask, pointing.

"Yes, the Pit of the Past. It includes all your lifetime experiences, knowledge, and opinions developed along the way. You have already seen it's best to not use the past to escape the present. It is a stinking place to lose oneself."

I smile.

"Many of those fearful of life live there," says the voice. "Yearning for what once was, but is no longer."

"The memories were so real!"

"Actually, they're not. We live as if our memories are accurate but in reality, they grow a little more distorted with each recollection. Far from perfect to begin with, the accuracy of any memory is further diminished in the retelling and reliving of it. And yet we live as if our memories are truths. The past shapes who you think you are and what choices you think you have in life. It's dangerous. Not only are memories inaccurate, but most of what you have come to believe simply is not so."

I notice several billowy clouds appear in the sky above the rocky peaks that now loom larger. My thoughts, which up until this point have not distracted me, start to creep in again. They gain in volume, both in the sound intensity and the number of successive thoughts.

"Eventually, thoughts can become habits or beliefs. Beliefs are no more than a persistent thought, slowly solidified over time, similar to how sediment accumulated over time becomes a rock. We think the thought so many times, it becomes solid, unmovable. Even though the thought may not be true, it becomes truth for us. Do you see those rocks in the Pit of the Past? Those are some of your beliefs."

What? I scrutinize the rocks, hoping to understand which beliefs they represent.

"But, just as with all of us, most of our rocks, or beliefs, are hidden from view. Some lurk below the surface or hide in the background, and we bump up against them time and time again. Others are right in front of our faces, but we don't see them."

"But, beliefs are good, aren't they?"

"You believe so!" says the voice. I note the point made.

"Beliefs can be useful. On troubled occasions your beliefs can be hugely sustaining and a source of certainty and clarity. Those are the few beliefs that are true for you down to your core. But most aren't like that. Most beliefs are things you were told that went unquestioned when you were young. Or they are conclusions you've prematurely drawn from a small and inadequate supply of information that you have ceased to examine for validity. You know, like the Imes and the Izzes."

I cock my head. "The imes and the izzes?" booms above at the same time I ask the question.

We both look up and laugh.

"Yes. The Imes and Izzes: conclusions drawn from inadequate information, sometimes formulated in just a few seconds, which we turn into beliefs. Someone says something insensitive, and we pronounce, 'She *is* mean.' A dropped dish turns into '*I'm* clumsy.' We live like our pronouncements are truths:

I'm this.

I'm not that.

Michael *is* this.

The world *is* such and such.

Erica *is* not that."

"We believe what we concluded with confidence and then

overlook, ignore, or reject new data that refutes our conclusions. Our Izzes and Imes become cemented in our thoughts, like rocks."

"Then one day, we are presented with evidence too strong to ignore that conflicts with our precious belief. Or we find ourselves doing something significant that conflicts with one of our beliefs. Or worse, we discover two of our beliefs contradict one another. BAM! All hell breaks loose."

"Is that what happened to me in the swamp of memories?"

"Yes. Very good! In the Pit of the Past. You were caught between a rock and a hard place."

We laugh.

"Do you know what two beliefs were at odds with each other in that moment?"

"I don't know!" the immediate thought sounds above. I observe the thought and let it go.

"Be still and look inside," the voice urges.

I pause, then redirect my attention inside to find my answer. I can feel the expanse inside my chest, my heart beating. After several minutes the answer wells up within me, without words. I just know.

"The belief that I should spend more time working toward my dream and the belief I will fail if I try. As soon as I promise to try, the fear I will fail shows up. I am afraid of failing and afraid of trying."

"What else do you notice?" asks the voice gently.

"That the turmoil is still there. I feel unsettled inside. Conflicted, dissonant, restless. I suspect I have felt this way for a very long time, but my awareness of it was only vague. It had no name. All I noticed was how exhausted I was. I can see now this was the source of my exhaustion—the struggle."

"Funny thing about the mind, it hates for beliefs to be questioned or challenged. The internal turmoil is tremendous as the mind attempts to reconcile the beliefs with the internal guidance of the heart. We think something external is causing the dissonance and something external will fix it. Sometimes we lie to ourselves in attempts to resolve the conflict. The heart knows the truth and will not let up until the lie is exposed."

"The heart?"

"Yes, the heart—the most important part of the You that you truly are."

9

Unmerry-Go-Round

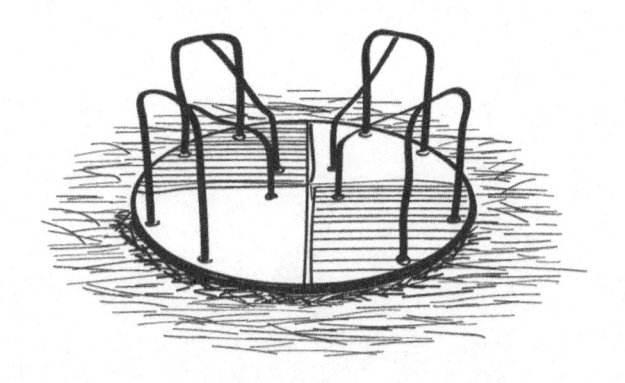

My eyes scan the landscape of my mind. I spy a merry-go-round over by the roller coaster, the kind you find in a park. The circular floor is a worn rusty red. The chipping paint on the bars is a faded taxi yellow. A wide, deep groove in the ground, where not a blade of grass grows, surrounds the platform. "A merry-go-round! How did I miss that?"

"Would you like to ride?" teases the voice.

"No, no, no! I am pretty sure I have ridden that thing many,

many, times. Don't tell me. It's the Last Word Merry-Go-Round where I prepare the same argument and clever responses in my head over and over and over again? Round and round and round?"

"Why, yes! That's what we do when we feel invalidated or treated unfairly. It's a fear-based reaction to feeling diminished. Sound familiar?"

"Oh, yes. I am a Has-To-Have-The-Last-Word and an I'm-Right-You're-Wrong kind of girl."

"So says the you that You forgot you are not," says the voice.

10

Hills and Holes

"So, what are those mountains over there?" I point to the countless mountains of varying sizes that extend to the horizon on my left.

"Those aren't mountains. Those are molehills."

"Oh."

"My molehills?"

"Yes."

"There are so many of them!"

"Yes."

My eyes move slowly from molehill to molehill. The commentary above me expresses amazement and shame at how much of my life was wasted fixating on matters of no consequence. From far away, I hear a moan. I do not speak. My thoughts announce my alarm at the distant noise, followed by my rationalization and conclusion it was just nothing.

"Why do I do that? Make mountains out of molehills?"

"A lack of confidence in ourselves and lack of trust in others causes the insignificant to rise in importance. We often take minor obstacles and amplify them with our fear. Ultimately, it's a fear-driven behavior based on a belief system rooted in a Mountain of Lies."

My gut winces with the last phrase, but I say nothing.

Several more clouds of doubt appear in the sky.

"Our response to fear comes in many forms," says the voice. "Look over there, at the foot of the closest molehills."

I scan the base surrounding the closest molehills. I don't see anything other than the massive evidence of my artistry to create problems where there are none. "I don't see anything."

"Let's get closer."

Sensing the instant shift in scenery, I spin around and almost lose, then catch my balance at the sandy edge of a bowling ball-sized hole. It starts to collapse under the weight of my foot. I step back.

I am now at the base of what was the closest molehill surrounded by piles of sand and twenty to thirty holes, some as big as graves, most big enough to fit a travel size suitcase, some holes recently dug, other diggings showing signs of age or abandonment.

"What are all these holes?"

"Empty ways we seek love, acceptance, and validation," says the voice. "We invest so much effort to please others, to win their approval and love. It's like digging holes in the sand, unending and futile. The hole just collapses into itself, never really accomplishing what is intended, the work never done."

I stand, pensive, and gaze at my work.

"All the digging in the world never gets us what we truly yearn," the voice continues. "Even if we meet success, the reward seems lacking because we are looking outside ourselves for validation—a place we will never find it. And so, we keep digging, trying to please, striving for approval, begging to be loved. It is fear perpetuating fear.

It leaves us frustrated, hurt, and eventually resentful that our efforts and sacrifices are not appreciated."

"Then, it is the Never-Ever, Bitter-Better," sighs the voice.

"Never, ever, bitter, better?"

"Sounds like a peanut butter cup!" sounds above. I shrug my shoulders and roll my eyes upward.

"Sorry. Ignore that."

"Yes. The Never-Ever, Bitter-Better cycle. When your efforts fail to please others, you either grow *bitter* and say, '*Never* again,' or you become more determined than *ever* to do *better*. Never-Ever, Bitter-Better!"

I smile in recognition of the familiar cycle.

"The hole you almost stepped in is for your boss. See the recent digging? There is Jackson next to it. Then your mom. Erica is closest to the tree to your left, next to your Dad. Those two big ones to your right are your sisters."

My eyes settle on the largest hole of all. I zig-zag around the other holes to stand at its edge. The hole is massive, irregular in shape as well as depth. There is a shovel lying near the rim. Freshly eroded sand from the contour of the outer wall forms a large peaked mound at the bottom near the farthest edge of the hole. Someone has done a lifetime of digging on this one. "Who is this?" I ask, not sure I want to know. "Michael?"

"No. Not Michael."

If not my ex-husband, who? Who did I work so hard to please and never succeed in winning their love and approval? In an instant, I know the answer. It comes as a sharp pain in my chest as the realization hits me hard.

"Me!"

I let out a sob and sink to my knees.

"It's me."

After a while, a flash of anger bolts through me. I stand up and brush the sand from my knees. I refuse to feel sorry for myself. I roughly wipe away my tears and turn my back on the incriminating display of my perpetual neediness.

Somewhere in the distance, I hear what sounds like a whimper and muffled crying. And then the sound is gone.

11

The Fruits We Bear

"Let's take a stroll," suggests the voice.

My thoughts proclaim my surprise and appreciation of the instant change to a new location. I am in the middle of an orchard, vibrant with the colors and sweet, earthy smells of an approaching harvest. The branches of the trees, laden with fruit, hang low. I survey my new landscape and marvel at row after row of the symmetrical staggered trees showcasing their sweet temptations. The simplicity and peacefulness of my new environment help to assuage my lingering upset over the useless, ugly holes. I inhale a deep breath and sigh. The intensity of the sigh surprises me.

My thoughts, muted above, speculate on why I am here, what possible dangers lurk between the trees, and then resume their usual commentary about my surroundings. I walk down the center of the orchard and notice the unique color of the fruit that has fallen to the ground.

"This is a refreshing change. Thank you," I say. "What kind of trees are these? I don't recognize their fruit."

"Why, it's the fruit of your labor, of course!" answers the voice.

"Oh! May I try one?" I say as I search for the perfect specimen to satisfy my curiosity.

"Of course. They are yours!" says the voice.

I pluck a multi-colored, peach-sized fruit from the tree, rub it on my clothing, and take a trusting bite. The booming *oohs* and *ahhs* above reveal my pleasure. "It is delicious!"

"We rarely stop to really enjoy the fruits of our labor. Once a task is complete, we move on to the next. We seldom pause to celebrate our achievements or acknowledge ourselves. Our fearful mind, believing the Mountain of Lies, minimizes and diminishes our contributions, hiding their true splendor, hiding *our* true splendor. Look around, Liza. These are your fruits. This is the difference you make in other's lives, your contributions to the world," says the voice.

"These are all mine? Surely not!"

"See what I mean?" says the voice.

We both laugh. I continue my walk. Row after row. My thoughts express my disbelief. How can all these contributions be mine?

"Touch the trunk of the tree," invites the voice.

I walk over and lay both palms on the nearest tree. My eyes grow wide. The image of a third grader I tutored when I was in eighth grade appears in my mind. He was a shy boy. He learned from my example, benefited from my consistency, encouragement, and attention for there was little at home. I draw my hands back in disbelief. There were no words, just the rich experience of acknowledgement, a knowing that I made a difference—even if I didn't know I did.

I run to the next tree and experience acknowledgement of my work as a bank teller when I was younger, and the multitude of little old men who would wait in line at my window, just because my smile brightened their day. More trees share gratitude for specific situations with my children, family, employers, clients, and co-workers—specific occasions where I offered encouragement, praise, or where my mere presence made a difference for another. Many are from store clerks and strangers I do not even recall. Some were big moments. Most were little. I see how important small gestures of kindness can be.

Overwhelmed, I look to the eyes.

"I never knew."

"You never believed. Many times you were told."

"I couldn't hear it."

"Yes," agrees the voice.

Occasionally, I go up to another tree to receive its gift and then continue my walk. I am joyous. I feel acknowledged, profoundly satisfied, and fulfilled. I walk in peace and listen to my thoughts share my reflections.

Wait a second. Something has changed but I am not sure what. I stop my walk and turn slowly in a circle as I try to put my finger on what is different. My thoughts grow louder.

"There is no fruit on these trees! Where is the fruit?"

I look closer. Some trees have no fruit whatsoever. Others bear only small, hard fruit that never ripened, either rotting on the tree or dropping to the ground green and inedible. My eyes dart to the eyes for an explanation.

"Often times we distract ourselves from what we really should be doing with our lives. We idle doing things that make us feel good about ourselves but do little to forward our growth. Or we create a safe little haven in which to hide. Fear of rejection, fear of loss, fear of failure guides our actions. We play safe, and when we do, our lives bear little fruit."

The impact of these words hits me like a gut punch. I swerve around to see the countless trees, the row upon row upon row of fruitless trees. "These are all mine?" I demand. My voice is shrill. "I did that?" My enraged thoughts go wild above me.

"The molehills! The holes! The barren trees! I am so stupid!" I shriek.

And then suddenly I am gone.

12

The Punishing Room

Where am I? I cringe in fear, not knowing what to do or where my thoughts have taken me. It is darker than dark, blacker than anything I have ever experienced. I hear an unbearable wail. Someone is in pain at the hand of another.

I slide down the hard, damp wall, drop my head to my knees, wrap my arms around my calves, and stick my fingers in my ears in an unsuccessful attempt to block out the sounds. Malevolent whispers, enraged shouting, blows, begging, crying, and wails of pain echo against the walls. I am certain the one crying is female. She sounds like a young woman or a girl.

Terrified yet compelled to do something, I gather my courage. Slowly, carefully, I use my hands and feet to test the ground ahead of me as I move in the direction of the commotion. After what seems like weeks, a sliver of light shines ahead. I edge toward it, filled with dread of what lies ahead. My heart pounds so loud in my chest I am certain it can be heard. I squeeze my eyes closed, hold my breath, and stand for an eternity trying to muster the nerve to take a quick peek into the space around the corner.

The woman's ceaseless whimpering haunts me.

I can take no more.

I peek around the corner and quickly withdraw back. A single lantern stands on a flat rock. The irregular surface of the wet walls and freakish shadows thrown by nubby stalactites reveal I am in a cave with at least two others, a formidable figure with their back turned to me and a woman wearing a hooded cloak that hides her face.

"You idiot! You stupid, stupid idiot!" the person with their back turned to me hisses. The voice sounds familiar but I cannot place it.

I peep around the corner again.

The tormentor has a woman's figure and dark hair. She raises her hand and strikes the other. The woman with the hooded cloak tries to get away but cannot escape the blow. She yelps in pain.

"How?" shrieks the aggressor, punching and holding the other by her hair under the hood.

"Can," punching her again.

"You," punching her again.

"Be," punching her again.

"So," punching again.

"Stupid?" she shrieks with a final blow. The figure in the cloak falls to the floor, sobbing. Unmoved, the dark-haired woman moves toward the crumpled body and kicks her.

No one deserves this. Ever. I forget my cowardice. "Stop!" I shriek, "Stop!"

The dark haired woman spins around in surprise, her cruel fist drawn back and her face full of hatred. I freeze as I stare into the eyes of myself. It is my voice! She is me! My thoughts reel as I face my biggest nightmare. How can this be? How can this monster be me? Who do I hate so much to treat so horrendous?

I look to the floor. The hood falls away to reveal the face of the one so stupid and worthy of punishment. The lady's lip is bleeding.

One eye is beginning to swell shut. Her dark hair clings to her tear-stained face. She is, unmistakably, also *me*.

My eyes move from Liza the unmerciful to the hated imperfect Liza crumpled on the floor. The truth and magnitude of what is happening and the lifetime it has been going on sinks in, no longer possible to deny. My legs give way underneath me. Howls of my despair echo throughout the cave.

Why? Why? Why? Why would I do this to myself? And why would I let myself continue to do it?

"Because you are afraid," whispers the voice.

13

Mountain of Lies

I am still on my knees but no longer in the cave. I look up at the eyes.

"I beat myself up."

"Yes. You can be quite the little tyrant."

I laugh despite my fatigue, grateful for the humor and relieved not to be bound by shame. "I sure can."

"It is your fear-based strive for perfection. It looks like you are fighting yourself when underneath it is a fierce battle between the heart and the Mountain of Lies," says the voice. "Look over there at the volcano! Look how much of your mind is taken up by the Mountain of Lies—the very core of your belief system! Liza, you believe the most horrendous of lies."

I look up at the ominous volcano and shiver although I am not cold. "What are the lies?" I ask, afraid of the answer, but no longer able to avoid the question. I brace myself for the truth.

"They are the imagined constraints that do not exist, falsehoods acting as unquestioned truths, your *shoulds* and *should nots*, your *musts* and *must nots*, and the most powerful and debilitating lies of all, the Ins and Uns."

"The Ins and Uns?" my thoughts ask. I say nothing.

"Yes, the Ins and the Uns:

The world and your resources are *in*adequate.

You are *in*sufficient.

You are *in*capable.

You are *in*dentured. Never free to do what you choose.

These are all lies.

And the Uns:

You are *un*attractive.

You are *un*worthy.

**And you are *un*deserving of love."

I nod in recognition of the undercurrent of my thinking, hidden yet omnipresent. To hear them spoken aloud is shocking. Inside a sea of emotions churns.

"You do not want to believe the things you hold as true, yet you have collected a *mountain* of evidence to prove they are. Your deepest fear is that the Ins and Uns lies are true," continues the voice.

"They are true!" my thoughts shout.

In that instant, I am back in the cave. I watch the monstrous version of myself hiss at the condemned me crumpled on the floor, "They are not lies! You *are* insufficient. You will *never* be enough! You are worthless! And you are not loved. You are not worthy of love and you never will be!" She punches the other me.

The cloaked Liza ducks and covers her head with her arms to block the blow. The punch lands squarely on her back and knocks her forward. She scrambles away to increase the distance from her tormentor, then turns to me with a desperate plea for help and panic on her face. "You *know* the truth, Liza. You *know!*" she cries.

Her cry sounds young, like a child. I look at the woman's face and see the fear of a child in the woman's eyes. I swerve to face the monster and am stunned to see the same childlike fear in her eyes, and I recognize the fear as my own. I feel a stabbing pain in my heart. In that moment I know their pain and suffering are caused by fear. My fear. Their acts are my acts, as a violent aggressor striking out in frustration, a victim too paralyzed to stand up for herself, and everything in between. Moved by the intimate understanding of the suffering before me, I forgive them both, an act of compassion that automatically extends to myself. In that split-second moment of grace, I know the truth. I know with certainty and I am amazed I ever doubted.

The ground rumbles beneath us.

"No!" I scream above the noise. "We are all worthy! We are all enough! We are all free! And beautiful. Each of us is magnificent in our own way! And never, ever doubt, WE ARE LOVED BEYOND MEASURE!"

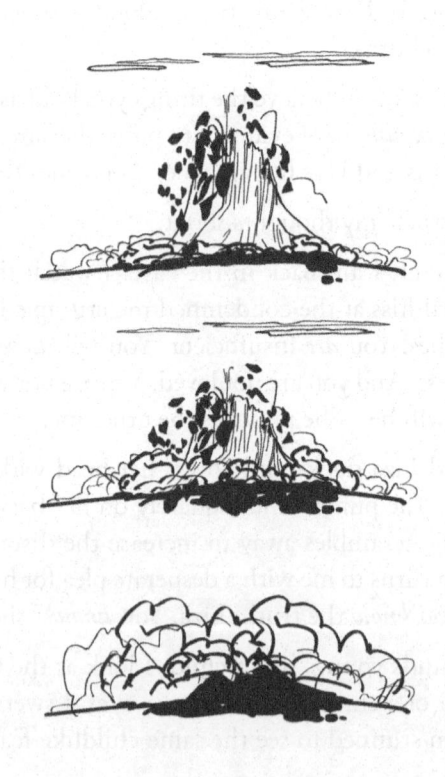

As the ground rumbles beneath my feet, I feel myself again transported. A half-second later I stand at the far edge of my mind watching the volcanic Mountain of Lies collapse, a magnificent sight that would normally instill terror in my heart. I feel no fear. I watch in awe.

"The heart won this one," says the voice.

"Yes," I say and smile.

14

The Bottomless Prayfors

Now sitting on plush grass, I watch the smoke and billow of dust clouds settle where the Mountain of Lies once towered.

"She said I knew the truth. But I didn't know I knew," I say, in great effort to sort out what just happened.

"Yes."

"And the next instant I just knew."

"Yes, the heart spoke and called in the real muscle to get things done."

I cock my head in surprise.

"Your Bottomless Prayfors."

"My bottomless what?"

"Your Bottomless Prayfors."

In that instant, three wells appear in a circle around us.

"Ah! Here they are! Divine timing! As always!" crows the voice with delight.

The first well is solid and sturdy. Heavy stones fit together in a tight circle. There are two thick forked limbs planted in the earth on either side. A wood beam sits squarely between the forks and stretches over the center of the well. A wooden bucket drawn from a pulley, full to the brim, sways ever so slightly as it dangles from the rope coiled around the beam.

"This one is Inner Strength."

I lean over the well into the tunnel of refreshing darkness. I sense the depth of the well reaches to eternity. I take a sip from the bucket and feel an immediate boost in my vitality, self-confidence, and determination. I recognize the feeling.

"It was Inner Strength that also welled within me in the Pit of the Past— when I thought my situation was hopeless."

"Yes."

"You could have taken the easy way out, but oh no, not you!" the voice teases.

We laugh.

"I am curious. What *is* the easy way out when you are lost in the past?" I ask.

"Gratitude for the present! Being grateful for what you have here and now."

"Of course!" I say, "Very good to know!"

We return our attention to the sturdy well.

"Inner Strength is always available when you need it."

We turn to the second well.

"This is Inner Peace."

The wall of the well and the small roof above it are made of corrugated metal. The well shimmers in the sunlight like a mirage in the desert. Sometimes I see the well clearly. Other times the well melts into the surroundings, no longer visible.

"Inner Peace is always here if you seek. But seek, you must."

I realize it is my desire to see that determines the well's visibility. If my attention shifts to anything else, the well is almost invisible. The well is there, but unseen. Unseen, unfelt. But there. Waiting.

I seek. The well comes into clear view. Not sure how I did it, I ask, "How do I seek Inner Peace?"

The eyes look surprised. "Why seek what is always already here?"

Now it is my turn to be surprised. "If Inner Peace is always, already here, what is it that I must seek?"

"You seek to remove your barriers that prevent you from experiencing it."

"Oh." I pause.

"What are my barriers?"

I know the answer before I complete the question and blurt out, "My thoughts!" at the same time the voice replies, "Your thoughts!"

"Jinx!'" we both shout. "You owe me a Coke!"

Of course. My thoughts, the ones I cling to instead of letting go!

My judgments, concerns, and distractions! These are my self-created barriers to Inner Peace.

I lean to take a small sip from the metal bucket. As soon as the liquid touches my lips, profound stillness calms every fiber of my being. Looking down, I catch my mirror-like reflection in the still water of Inner Peace. I drop a small stone into the well and watch as it hits the surface of the water. Not a splash or a ripple. Not even a sound. Smooth as glass. The stone, embraced by the water, sits quietly at the bottom of the pool. The water is undisturbed.

A divine demonstration of what's possible when barriers are removed.

Goosebumps rise in a standing ovation.

I bask in the perfect stillness until Inner Peace melts again into my surroundings.

We turn to the last of the Bottomless Prayfors. Unlike the others, this well is a beautiful urn-shaped tank with a copper pump and spigot.

"And this is Inner Wisdom."

The well disappears. I jump in surprise. The voice laughs. "Inner Wisdom has a collective mind of its own."

The urn and copper pump with spigot pop back into view. Then out. I watch in amazement.

"Inner Wisdom pops in and out as she pleases," says the voice. "She arrives, unbidden to deliver insight and helpful tidbits that can prove pivotal in the direction we take in life. Then, poof! She is gone! Her favorite thing is to inspire ideas and accompany a rush of creativity. She is unpredictable! Unconstrained! After all, who can put limits on the attainment of wisdom!"

I smile. The next time the well appears, I take a sip of her ancient elixir and experience a moment of epiphany. Then another. My eyes spring wide open as I receive flashes of insight.

"The waters of the Bottomless Prayfors are inexhaustible. Their gifts arrive unexpected, miraculously timed, and always welcome!"

"Is there a way I can access their remarkable powers?" I ask.

"Inner strength. Inner peace. Inner wisdom. They're what we pray for!" says the voice.

Ah. So, they are.

"You may never see them again. But trust they are always here. For you."

"Thank you!" I say to the wells with my arms extended high in an air hug.

I can no longer see them, but I know they are there.

15

Knowledge & Knowing

"So, what thoughts did Inner Wisdom share with you?" asks the voice.

"I can open myself to other ways of *knowing*."

The voice is quiet. I go on.

"And I should listen to my heart."

"Ah, yes. There is knowledge and *knowing*. And then there's trust."

We both laugh.

"Don't say the T word!" my thoughts jest above.

Seriously, how do I *know*, I mean, like really *know*?" I ask.

"Well, you are familiar with the traditional acquisition of knowledge. Facts and more facts. Knowledge evolves as new discoveries are made. Your knowing is based on what you have learned or experienced."

I nod my head in understanding.

"And then there is a second kind of knowing, a recognition of what's true for you. It is an experience of certainty—absolute, timeless and constant. This kind of knowing arises in the moment, such as the gifts from Inner Wisdom. What is newly discovered is not learned. The insight is a gift supplied to you and for you. You just *know* it."

"Fact vs. feeling?" I ask.

"It's much deeper than a feeling. You are certain of the rightness of it to the depth of your core. Nothing resonates like truth. We have an innate ability to recognize truth, when we hear it and when we feel it."

"Like intuition."

"Intuition is Inner Wisdom combined with emotional guidance from the heart. It, too, can be trusted for the heart speaks only truth."

"And how do I know it is the heart speaking?"

"Emotion is the language of the heart. The experience of freedom and joy are the heart's favorite way to speak to you—to confirm you are on a path true to who You really are."

"And if I am not in alignment?" I ask.

"The heart's sole purpose for communication is to make sure your thoughts and actions are aligned with who You really are and to redirect you when they are not. Behind every emotional discomfort, there is a thought that is out of alignment with your heart."

"All emotional discomfort?"

"Yes," says the voice. "Just as physical pain is a clue something is wrong with your body, emotional discomfort is your first clue that your thinking is out of alignment with the heart. If you act in accordance with an offending thought, your emotional discomfort increases. The heart is relentless. Discomfort disappears only when alignment with who You truly are is restored. Ignore it and the discomfort never goes away."

I nod and marvel at the simplicity. Discomfort? Rethink.

Realign. No more discomfort. My thoughts quiet in recognition of its importance. I must remember this.

"The unease is a gift! It is your cue to question your thinking and pinpoint the fear driving the thinking. Expose the lie and you are freed! Align with the heart and you will experience joy! Eliminate fear and you will always, *always*, be returned to love. The heart is the voice of the You that you truly are."

"And, I can trust the voice of who I truly am," I say and release a tremendous sigh of gratitude and relief. My words resonate as truth the moment I say them. I feel the certainty down to my core. Joy bursts with the realization that *there is a part of me I can trust!* I was right to distrust the voice inside my head, but I didn't know where to turn! I was lost. My thoughts shout happy victories, "I can trust myself! I can trust myself!"

I feel myself grow bolder.

"Yes," says the voice. "You will hear the heart speak most clearly when fear and busyness are set aside. But you will miss the messages from Inner Wisdom, intuition, and the heart if you are not open and aware. Or you will shrug them off if you do not believe."

"I believe. How do I stay open and aware?"

"Your receptivity is greatest when you are seated behind your thoughts."

The eyes catch my quizzical look and explain.

"In life, you can either be in your thoughts or behind them. When you are in your thoughts, there is no distinction between you and them. You and your thoughts are one and the same. You are your thoughts, your emotions, and your body sensations. This perspective lacks objectivity."

"That is mostly what I do."

"It is mostly what *you used to do*," the voice corrects.

I smile and nod.

"You are most effective in life when you get behind your thoughts—distance yourself from them. From this perspective, you are present and can observe your mind at work. You see your thoughts and emotions as they appear, hear your self-talk, observe your body sensations, and view the activity of people and things around you. You are aware."

"I stay in the Now."

"Yes."

"And if I am observing, I will be able to easier recognize truth arise because I am not fixated or distracted by my mind's chatter! I can't hear as well when I am on the worry coaster, or digging holes in the sand, or making molehills!"

"Yes! The messages arise either way. It is a matter of whether you listen and recognize them. It is in the calmness, seated behind your thoughts that you will best know when your Inner Wisdom, intuition, or heart speaks. You develop the skills to listen for them through practice. And you will *know* to trust them."

"It is also here, seated behind my thoughts, I can best make my own alignment corrections. Adjust my thinking. Right?"

"Yes!"

"How do I get rid of the bad thoughts?"

"Once thunk, you cannot unthink a thought!"

I smile.

"The thunk thought cannot be erased or destroyed. To regret or resist an undesirable thought only gives it more power. The harder you try to push the thought away, the longer it will linger."

"So, what do I do?"

"Abandon the thought the instant you deem it undesirable."

"But how? I have tried to stop thinking about something before. I can never do it!"

"Intentionally think a new, worthy thought—one that serves you. Focus your attention and energy there."

I nod. "And the undesirable thought will lose its pull on me and disappear?"

"Yes, in proportion to your level of inattention to one and the momentum in activity to advance the other. It is best to fortify the new worthy thought by taking action consistent with the intention. The quicker, bigger, and more frequent the action, the stronger the new thought will become!"

"Action gives the new thought more power?"

"Yes. Without it, the new thought will languish."

"Will I get a chance to practice?" I ask with the slyest of grins to match my obvious hint. I am eager to return home.

"Indeed."

My heart leaps. Happy thoughts zing through the air.

The eyes narrow, eyebrows furrow. "You're not going home wearing that, are you?" A joke.

I am confused but retort, "Oh, now you're my fairy godmother?"

"Today I am. We need to lighten you up!"

And off we go to another alcove in my mind.

16

The Closet of My Mind

We stand in a dim corridor in front of the door of an enormous vault. My thoughts chatter of secrets and discovery. I am giddy with the promise of going home. Everything is beautiful.

"Where are we?"

"We are outside the closet of your mind. Here is where the thoughts you select, collect, and protect reside."

"Thoughts I select, collect, and protect?"

"Yes, the thoughts you adopt as your own to build the identity and behaviors of the you that you forget you are not."

The air feels weighty. My cheer runs away to hide. Unsure of myself, I look to the eyes. "Shall I open the door?"

"Only you know how!" chuckles the voice. The lightness returns.

The heavy door creaks open to reveal a comfortable antique filled room. The moment I cross the threshold every fiber of my being recognizes the feeling of this room although I have never seen it. My thoughts speculate on its familiarity.

I look around. The room is pure Liza. Only things I love,

admire, or once longed for fill the room. The floor is covered with a Tabriz Persian carpet. One wall is lined with several antique armoire wardrobes polished to show off the grain of the wood. At the end of the room, opposite the door, stands a matching full-length three-panel mirror and a clothes tree. An intricate dividing screen partitions off the back corner.

The lighting is soft and inviting. To my left sits a comfortable leather chair with a hand-made lap quilt folded over one arm. Next to the chair is a rotating glass case. With each turn, something magnificent is displayed and is replaced with something equally extraordinary at the next turn. A colorful hand-blown glass teapot makes its pass in a graceful circle. I remember it from an art gallery when I was young. The teapot is followed by a mesmerizing sculpture of two lovers, a hand-turned wood kaleidoscope, and a quirky topsy-turvy house molded by a famous potter. Art that fascinates and moves me adorns the walls. I couldn't buy them or have them, so I took them with me to my mind. All of these things are a part of me, thoughts and memories of things that shaped who I believe myself to be or aspire to be. *Oohs* and *ahhs* sound in appreciation.

"I know this place. This is where I go to escape or think. To find solace."

"Or brood."

I laugh. "Yes, that too."

An ornate built-in bookcase lines the entire wall to my right. From my waist down are hand carved cabinets with multiple drawers. I walk over and pull one of the handles. The drawer slides open to reveal its function: a filing cabinet. Curious, I look to see what I have filed. In the first drawer, I see my Imes and Izzes neatly organized. My eye catches one that I am certain is not true. I pull it from the drawer. It disappears. I pull more. They disappear too.

Like a voyeur, I peruse the thoughts that are filed in my mind's cabinet. In them, I rediscover an appreciation for the uniqueness of this me who is crafted by thought. My imperfections. My inconsistency in tastes. My playfulness and quirks.

In each drawer I open, I find and remove thoughts inspired by fear. In one drawer, buried at the bottom, I find countless sorrows hidden away. I toss them all and watch them disappear. I feel lighter.

On a few occasions, I feel the pull of the Pit of the Past begin to take me away as I engage with a memory. I stop myself and get present.

The eyes watch, patient.

There are too many thoughts for me to review. It would take years. Appeased for now, I close the drawer and look up to see an original Dr. Suess painting among the work of masters. I laugh. The incongruity is so me! I could choose anything and I chose Suess!

Mouth ajar, I marvel at Horton and the little Who, my favorite reminder that we each have a voice no matter how small—a thought I latched onto as a child that became a part of who I am. The freedom of new insight spreads tingles throughout my body. I get it. I get it! The hair on my arms prickles in a wave.

"I can select any thought to shape my self!" I cry out and turn to the eyes.

"Yes!" affirms the voice. "Any thought you choose!"

"I didn't know."

"And, now, you do!"

"But more of my thoughts have got to go!"

"Yes, Liza. Next time a thought appears that is no longer to be yours, let it go. It is a practice."

17

Insults, Injuries & Injustices

My thoughts return to my desire to go home. *I need something to wear. Isn't that why I am here?* I walk to the wardrobe closest to the vault entrance and swing both doors wide open. In the center compartment, there are two hooks. One holds a full suit of armor. The second hook is empty. Drawers and cubbies store ballistic vests, medieval weapons, replacement armor parts, and adjustment tools for the armor.

Armor? Suits of armor? Ballistic vests? My thoughts go crazy. *I don't collect armor! I don't even like it. It's for war!*

I rush to the center armoire, the largest and most ornate of the three wardrobes. The heavy doors creak as they swing open.

"No clothes!" my thoughts announce.

Within the center section of the wardrobe sits a large scoreboard. *A scoreboard?*

"**I**nsults, **I**njuries & **I**njustices to Liza," the scoreboard reads.

"Insults, injuries, and injustices," my thoughts repeat aloud.

"Ah, you count your I's!" says the voice.

I study the tally of the I's I received from others over the years. Michael tops the list with the most points. Family members compete for most of the other top spots. Co-workers and friends vie for a poor third.

"I guess I do. My mother always said I did," I concede.

"Many of these are imagined crimes committed against the you that you forgot you are not, sold to you as true by the Mountain of Lies." I bristle at the word *imagined* and cringe at the mention of the Mountain of Lies.

"Imagined! What do you mean, *imagined*!" my thoughts roar. The tone matches my fury over the insinuation.

I say nothing. A dark green coin falls from the air and I catch it, an act so natural, so instinctive, I am certain I have done it a thousand times. Looking up, I see no clue to its origin. I shrug and tuck it in my pocket. To my surprise, I discover more than a handful of coins already there.

"Another grievance for your collection!" says the voice.

"Collection?" I ask. The eyes meet my gaze and roll toward

the drawers of the opened wardrobe. I follow the eyes. Each drawer is labeled. The ones to the left of the scoreboard are labeled "GRIEVANCES," as are all but the two bottom drawers on the right. Those two are labeled "GRUDGES." Hmm. I have more grievances than grudges.

My thoughts make wisecracks. "Oh great! I am a hoarder of complaints and resentments!"

I open a drawer. It is heavy with green coins identical to the ones in my pocket. I guess I am.

"Your collection of G's," explains the voice. "Your grievances and grudges. We collect them and carry them with us as if they hold some future value, but they never do. They only weigh us down."

The green coin feels heavy in my hand. I know what grievance it represents. I toss it to the floor. It disappears. I feel lighter. The eyes light up with approval. I grab handfuls of coins from the drawer, toss them down, and watch them disappear as they hit the floor. "I don't need these!" I shout and proceed to discard my grievances.

After a while I ask, "Why are some coins much heavier than others?"

"The weight of the coin is equivalent to the burden we feel and the strength of our justification to keep it. The more we hate, fear, or avoid, the heavier the coin. The irony is if you do not toss the coin, the very situation you resist or avoid is bound to recur. That gives your grievance even more weight."

"And the probability it will show up again."

"Yes. A coin is easier to toss early on and becomes heavier and more difficult to toss the longer you keep it."

My arms tire so I select the lightest ones and continue to toss them to the floor. Is the lightness I experience when the coins disappear real or imagined? My thoughts quibble over the answer. I sense it is real.

Soon, only the heavy grievance coins remain.

Next, I empty the bottom drawers of all but the heaviest of grudges. I strain to pick one up. The recognition of the grudge comes easy. My temper flares as a wave of righteousness flows through me. I am not quite ready to retire my role as victim. My thoughts justify my decision to leave the coin in its place. I shut the drawer.

"Maybe not today," encourages the voice. This generous absence of judgment makes room for self-compassion. I recognize it as the detour away from the punishing room. I take it.

18

Context Lenses

We move to the last armoire. My thoughts express my hopes for clothes and not another surprise. I open the doors. Row upon row of identical pairs of eyeglasses peer out at me. On the inside of each door is a mirror. What a strange place for an optical shop!

"What are all these?"

"Designer lenses."

"Designed by who?" I ask.

"Why, you, of course! By the thoughts you select to entertain rather than let go!"

"But I don't even wear glasses!"

"Oh, but you do! We all view life through lenses and think we do not."

Sure enough, I catch my reflection in the mirror on my right, and I *am* wearing glasses. Multiple pairs!

"Do these help me see?"

"Just the opposite. The lenses limit what you can see to *only* what you believe and make you blind to the truth. Here, let me show you. Try on the first pair of glasses on your left and look into the other mirror."

"Surely they won't fit!" cry my thoughts.

They do.

The new glasses stay in place over the others I am already wearing. I look into the mirror and see an earlier version of myself during a dark period of my life after my college boyfriend ended our relationship. The misery and the hopelessness of that period fill me. I feel like I can't go on without him.

"Now remove the lenses, watch for a bit, then place them back on again," instructs the voice. "Notice the contrast."

With one hand, I tilt the temple of the spectacles up so that the nose bridge rests on my forehead. It's subtle, but the despair is gone. I am still miserable, but not hopeless. The scene shifts. I open Erica's bedroom door. She is huddled on the floor, her cell phone near her. "He broke up with me!" she wails. I am sympathetic and want to comfort her.

I let the glasses fall back onto the bridge of my nose. The hopelessness returns. How could this happen? My daughter will never be happy again! I lift the spectacles up. The hopelessness disappears. I am empathetic and almost amused that my daughter thinks this is the end of her life. Spectacles back down. My life was ruined and now hers will be too.

I snatch the lenses from my face. "This is ridiculous!"

"What is the context of the lens? Can you determine the belief distorting your perspective?"

"That somehow my happiness depends on someone else! Or that Erica's happiness does!"

"Yes. There was a time this was true for you. You believed your happiness depended on the love of another. Do you remember?"

"I do. It took me years to figure out my happiness was not tied to him or anybody else. Only I can generate happiness for myself."

"When you figured that out, you stopped wearing these."

"Oh," I say and lay the glasses down on the shelf.

"Shall we take a look at one of the lenses you wear now?"

I look in the mirror and watch as various scenes of my life, my work, and my family play out. I don't notice anything in particular. Then I lift the most outward pair of lenses up. There is an immediate shift in the way I feel. It's hard to describe what is changed. I let the glasses fall back down on my nose. I feel…what is it? I feel lonely. I lift the glasses back up. The loneliness disappears. I try again. No, I don't think it's loneliness. I feel isolated, abandoned. I lift the glasses up again.

"When I wear these, I feel abandoned. Isolated."

"So what is the lens through which you view things? How does life *seem* to you?"

"It seems like I am all alone. I have no one to turn to."

"Is it true?" the voice implores.

I look into the mirror again.

My mother suggests we take a day off to shop. I am too busy. Too busy at work and too busy to see what is really going on. I hear the concern in her voice for the first time. I see the concern in her eyes. I watch the disappointment cross her face as I shoot the idea down. She knows! My mom knows I am struggling with something although I intimated nothing. I see it!

The lenses go back down. I see what I always see. I am so busy and all my mom can think about is me taking a day off to take her shopping.

"No! Oh my gosh! Mom!" I wail. "I am so sorry!" I turn to the eyes. "I never saw it! I swear!"

"You couldn't. When you view life through this lens, love and support are not possible. Your view through the lens becomes your reality. You are blind to the truth that support is and has always been here, ready and waiting for you to accept. From your mom and countless others."

The truth resonates in my ears like only truth can do. I am not alone. Support *has* always been there. Joy. Remorse. Hurt for my mom. Hurt for me. I don't know what emotions swell within me. There are too many.

"It starts as an innocent observation. It seems like... We gather evidence that the way we view life is true. Thought becomes belief. Then we align our actions through the lens of our new truth."

"But the perspective isn't the truth. It's a lie!"

"Yes, but we are blind to the lie. Our belief becomes an undetected distortion we use to taint the interpretation of everything that we see and experience around us. And we don't even realize we are doing it. We believe it's just the way life *is*. But it is only the lens we use to view things."

Just a lens! Not the truth! The words sink in. I feel imaginary shackles on my hands and feet break open and fall to the floor. I stand taller.

"If we view life through the lens of '*The world is dangerous*,' we lead small lives. We cut ourselves off from true love and connection with the lens of '*I can't trust anyone*.' Peace and happiness are unavailable when we look through the lens of '*It shouldn't be this way*.' A lens of '*I can't have what I want!*' yields a life of frustration and resentment. '*I don't belong*' causes us to hide, shrink back, and withhold the gift of our self-expression from the world."

"I am probably wearing some of those context lenses too!"

"All lenses are a barrier to love and tinted by the Mountain of Lies."

"I can see that," I say.

"No pun intended! Shall we try another?" asks the voice.

I look in the first mirror and pick from the multiple pairs of glasses I already wear. I push one pair up to rest on the top of my head and turn toward the other mirror, that lens off. An image of my mother's kitchen comes into focus. The wilted ivy cutting in a neglected glass of water on the windowsill above the sink makes me laugh. My mother is always trying to grow things in that window. Despite the fact the plants are in full view, they often die from inattention. She doesn't see them. A round, three-tiered chocolate cake sits on the counter, my mother's signature dessert for her children, now all grown. I notice a smear where frosting is missing along the bottom. Someone has succumbed to the temptation of taking a small taste without my mother's knowledge. My dad's unfinished crossword puzzle lies on the counter next to the cake, a clue left in haste to avoid detection.

My gaze settles on the scuffed up walnut drop-leaf dining table. I spent countless hours at this table, laughing, joking, reminiscing, and exchanging gossip with family and friends. Michael and I sat at this table when we told my mom and sisters I was pregnant with Erica. My dad stunned us with an unusual display of emotion. Actual tears.

This table is where my sisters and I did our homework at night, When we were teenagers, instead of doing our work, we whispered which boy was the last to kiss us, a game we played, sometimes a lie, sometimes true. Our howls of laughter climbed to hysteria until my dad yelled from the living room for us to be quiet, which only set off another bout of uncontrolled giggles. It is here we shared our most intimate woes. And victories. It's where my mom chose to tell us girls she had cancer. Like a mama sea turtle that instinctively knows thirty years later to return to the same beach where she was hatched to lay her own eggs, I instinctively know to come here, to this table, when I am wounded, sad, or unsure of myself. I come here for a different kind of nourishment, to heal, to surround myself with those who love me, often unbeknownst even to myself that I am doing so.

I realize now, my sisters do the same thing. An invisible thread weaves an unbreakable bond between us all. The bond is always there, rarely acknowledged, often denied.

A tsunami of emotions rises and catches me off guard as I think of my family. A sob erupts without warning. I am unable to contain or stop it.

The eyes are patient.

"I'm sorry."

Embarrassed, I try to stop crying, but there is so much more from wherever these emotions rise.

"I'm sorry. I don't know why I am doing this."

"Let the emotions rise. Fully experience them and let them go. Attach no meaning."

I do my best to follow the odd advice. I am accustomed to suppressing deep emotions, not letting them show. They scare me.

After a bit, I collect myself.

"I'm sorry."

"I don't know why I keep saying I'm sorry!"

Quiet.

"Sheesh! That certainly snuck up on me! All that fuss over a kitchen table!"

We laugh.

"I keep telling my mom to get rid of it! It was given to her before I was born!"

The eyes smile.

"I didn't realize it until now; I come to my mother's kitchen to sort things out. I was here almost every week for months after Michael left."

I sniff and dry my tears.

"Ok, I'm ready." With reluctance, I put the glasses back down on the bridge of my nose. I watch another scene unfold in the mirror.

My mom, Chrissy, Gina, and I sit at the kitchen table. It has been months since we last saw one another. Our children are in the living room playing. Nothing unusual.

I am struck by the absence of the tenderness I felt only moments ago and how fast I shifted to the passive mood I experience now. The lens is at work.

I raise the glasses up. I feel my body relax. My tenderness for my family returns.

Lenses back down. My body tenses. My eyes narrow, wise in the ways of female competition. As the innocent banter progresses, a silent comparison is conducted at all levels. I feel my appearance and mood studied with my mother's and sisters' gaze. My level of confidence is evaluated when I laugh. We exchange updates on our families and lives. The scoring continues. Who has gained or lost weight? Who looks prettier? Are those the same boots she wore last year? Whose career is advancing with the most momentum? Who is happier? The smaller threat I pose, the fewer conversational barbs, disguised as jest, will be thrown my way.

I lift the glasses up. The competitiveness disappears. I feel safe, loved, and connected. I look at the women in my family with fondness and bask in their affection for me.

The glasses fall back on the bridge of my nose. My body reacts. Shoulders tense with the accumulation of decades of hurt and anger. I shrink back and make myself small. My imaginary wall rises.

"I am protecting myself!"

"Yes. What else?"

Gina and Chrissy burst out laughing. Are they laughing at something or someone? Anyone not present is open game. My judgment squashes my affection for them.

"Now they are dangerous."

I lift the glasses up. "Now they are not."

The wall disappears. It is just my sisters and me enjoying our lifelong competition of wit. Laughter is my favorite music and they are playing one of my favorite songs.

The glasses go down. I sense the conversation turning injurious. We each know just what to say to hurt the other and will not hesitate to do so if we feel justified. I watch their every move, prepare to dodge their barbs and inflict my own. I am critical of what I hear and see.

I don't like how I feel or who I am being.

I look harder. What am I hiding?

Yes, that's it. I am hiding that I am afraid of what they think of me. Fearful of their condemnation, I defend and attack. Chrissy and Gina laugh again. In an instant, I recall the shaping moment from fifth grade with Betsy and Claire. And my favorite shirt. The nature of the lens becomes clear.

"I don't trust them! They are judging me."

"Yes. Look closer. Who is doing the judging?"

I gasp. "Me! I think they are judging me. But it is me that is judging them!"

"Yes. You have been wearing and refining these lenses since you were ten years old."

"Fifth grade."

"Yes."

"I judge my mom, my sisters, my dad. I have diminished their love for me and shrunk away from fully expressing my love for them. For more than twenty years."

The eyes blink in understanding.

I bite my lip. Another tsunami brews within.

"I guess I do that to everybody, don't I?" But I know the answer. Mostly. Not always.

The voice is quiet.

I am quiet, too, as I grapple with the impact of this revelation. I talk in hushed tones to myself even though I know the voice can hear me. I don't want my thoughts announced above me to interrupt my chain of thought.

"I judge. I judge people. I judge circumstances. I judge things. Inferior. Superior. Better. Worse. Good. Bad. Right. Wrong. I judge at great cost to myself and everyone around me. I don't understand. I *hate* it when I think I am being judged! So, why do I always do it?"

I answer my own question. "Fear. It has to be fear. It always is, isn't it?"

The eyes are attentive, voice silent.

I continue thinking aloud. "I'm sure fear is at the core of judgment. The purpose of judgment is to detect and assess risk, right? It's a protection mechanism I wield like a sword, a skill I have honed to perfection. I'm even judging now. How well am I doing? Will I get the right answer? Even though I see I cannot truly love or be loved with judgment present, I still judge."

I stop talking and try to stop judging. My inner turmoil builds. My thoughts resume their overhead broadcast. I wish they would stop. Now I am judging my thoughts.

"I don't know how to stop!" I turn to the eyes for aid. "How do I stop judging?"

"You don't," the voice says calmly. "You can't."

It is not the answer I want or expected, but the truth rings true. My thoughts go berserk above me.

"But why?"

"It's in our nature to judge. Our brains are designed to assess, compare, analyze. It's what brains do. Judgments, after all, are only thoughts. They appear and will also disappear if we simply observe them. Judgments only achieve longevity if we give them attention and adopt them as truths."

I relax a little.

"Let the thoughts arise. Observe the judgment in them. And then let them go. Don't analyze the judgment to see if you agree or disagree. Just let it go. You can't stop your thoughts. What we all *can* do is choose to stop being judgmental."

"Oh," I say. I sigh with relief and then freeze.

"But I'm always judgmental!" sounds above.

I look up and then meet the eyes. I own my flaw. "I am very judgmental."

"Ah, the Imes and the Izzes strike again! You *believe* you are judgmental, Liza. You are not. Sometimes you *choose to be* judgmental. Sometimes you are asleep to the fact you are *being* judgmental. You may even be being judgmental by default, a habit developed over time such that it feels like the real you. It is not You. Being judgmental is a state. It's a choice. It is not permanent nor out of your control. It is 100% your responsibility at any given moment to be judgmental or not!"

"I think I understand."

"Understanding is the booby prize!" says the voice with a roar. "The gold is in the practice of choosing who or what you want to be in the moment! Besides, why choose to be judgmental? There are so many other exciting things to be!"

So it is me, and only me, that determines if I am being judgmental. Odd as it sounds, that little fact brings me supreme joy.

"How about one more set of lenses?" I ask.

The eyes study me.

"Pretty please! This is eye-opening," I jest.

The eyes oblige.

I pick another pair of glasses and turn to watch the scene play in the second mirror. It is summer, early evening. I am cooking dinner. I walk into the garage to get a gallon of milk from the second refrigerator. I smile upon my discovery that Michael has just arrived home. He is early! Although the engine of his car is off, the news blares from the radio.

I roll my eyes. I know this scene. It is the pivot point where my tolerance of Michael's controlling behavior ends and the unraveling of my marriage begins.

The smile disappears from my face as I realize I forgot to close the garage door again. Michael looks pissed. He sees me and flicks the radio off in one angry motion.

"Liza, you forgot to shut the garage door again. How many times do I have to tell you?"

I turn on my heels and storm into the house.

Years have gone by since that ugly afternoon, yet I flare in defensiveness as I watch the scene unfold. My neck stiffens and I clench my jaw. He is so frigging controlling. Always criticizing me. Always telling me what to do. This scene was the final straw. No, wait. The final straw was actually the next day when our neighbor knocked on the door and asked me to close the garage door. He said Michael asked him to remind me. *That* was the final straw.

The scene ends.

"Ok!" I say. "One more time!" I half growl.

With a dramatic snort, I lift the glasses from the bridge of my nose and place them to rest on the top of my head. Even though my anger disappears, my mood plummets. Anything that has to do with Michael wears me out. This time the same scene plays but it starts a few minutes earlier than the first time. While I watch I tear a hangnail on my thumb with my teeth.

The window of the old Mustang is down, music loud. Michael strums his fingers on the steering wheel to the beat of the song as he drives.

"I used to love to watch him do that," I say to the voice.

The song ends and the news broadcast begins as Michael turns into the alley.

"We just received breaking news that a third woman has been assaulted in the metroplex area." Michael turns the radio up, concerned and attentive.

I am confused. I look over to the eyes. "I don't remember any assaults. But I never listen to the news." I rip at another fingernail.

Details of the latest assault are announced, but I don't pay much attention. I am more interested in another benefit of having the lenses off. I miss looking at Michael and not feeling angry. It's nice. Really nice.

Michael waves to Mrs. Jackson as she opens her gate to take her dog for a walk.

Michael has such a great smile.

Up the alley, Michael notices our garage door is open. Again. He closes his eyes and groans.

I expect to start getting mad and defensive. But I don't. Not looking through lenses works!

One house before ours, Michael sees our next-door neighbor and stops the car. Michael shouts to Jeff. Jeff waves and trots over to the car to talk to Michael.

"Hey, Jeff, can you keep an eye on Liza for me? I just heard there was a third assault. First one was pretty close to here. I keep asking Liza to keep the garage shut and locked. But, as you can see, she forgot again today. If you see it open, please tell her I asked you to remind her to keep it closed. I don't want to scare her by mentioning the assaults. I just want her to be safe."

"Sure, Mike."

"Thanks, buddy. I appreciate it."

My eyes widen and I gasp out loud. There is ringing in my ears. Gray appears in the peripheral of my vision. Unsteady, I hold onto the armoire door for support. No! No. This can't be! What have I done? What have I done?

My stomach lurches. But I cannot free myself from the pull of the scene playing in the mirror. The washboard that has risen in my throat blocks my repeated attempts to swallow. I choke on the truth. I may have made a terrible mistake. If I was so clueless in this instance, how many other times did I misinterpret Michael's actions? Or the actions of others?

Michael puts the car back in gear and continues down the alley. He pulls the car into the open garage and shuts off the engine, then turns the key so he can listen to the end of the news broadcast.

It is anxiety, not anger, on his face.

"All three victims were assaulted in their own homes. None knew the perpetrator. In all three instances, there is no evidence of forced entry. Detectives are asking residents to keep their garage doors shut and..."

Michael looks up, sees me, and snatches off the radio.

An act of protection! He doesn't want me to be afraid!

"Liza, you forgot to shut the garage door again. How many times do I have to tell you?"

I watch in disbelief. I know my next move.

I turn on my heels and storm into the house.

I swerve around to face the eyes. "Not long afterward, I told Michael I didn't want to be married to him anymore. I thought he was critical and controlling about *everything*."

"How was he controlling?" the voice asks.

"Lots of ways. He was always telling me what to do." I hear myself say *always* and mentally wince. Whatever comes after that word is usually an exaggeration—a lie.

"He treated me like a child. He would always remind me when it was time for me to leave to go somewhere." *So I wouldn't be late*, I think to myself as the words leave my mouth.

"Or he would text me reminders of what to buy at the store." *So I wouldn't forget*, I think and don't say.

"Or he'd tell me it was time to put gas in the car—as if I didn't know! Or send me text reminders to take my lunch break at work." *Because I often get so focused I forget to eat.*

"Michael hates waste. So he was always nagging me to turn off the lights when I left a room," *because I often leave them on,* "or shut the door."

"He would even set out my vitamins or bring me my pill if I was sick to make sure I took my antibiotics the entire ten days! He was always telling me what to do and following after me!"

The more I try to explain, the more hollow my accusations sound.

"And a million other things!"

"Sounds dreadful!" the voice teases.

"I was so sure I was right! That he was controlling and fault-finding." I concede.

"Yes. It is a function of the lens to be righteous about your own point of view. We are so sure!"

"He didn't want to leave. I made him."

"Righteousness and being right can come at great cost."

"I told him I didn't love him. But it was a lie."

"Can you take responsibility for your actions?"

"Yes," I say.

And then I sob. Sorrow-filled. Long and hard. But I do not beat myself up or long for the past or fret about what will happen next. I just let myself be sad—for Michael, for my kids, and their sometimes critical, controlling, absent-minded mother.

At long last I stop and ask, "Want to hear something funny?"

I don't wait for an answer.

"After Michael left he trained Erica and Jackson to make sure the garage door was closed. I thought he did it to get back at me. And I caught him several times driving down the alley. I thought he was spying on me. *Aaaagh!* Why didn't he say something?"

But I know the answer.

My trembling hands reach up to remove the glasses. I am keen to be rid of the lenses. They do not budge. A quick look in the first mirror confirms my suspicion. Not only am I wearing the *"Michael is controlling"* lenses, I am wearing them all.

"The lenses through which you view your life cannot be removed here."

"I will practice until they disappear," I say with a fierceness that surprises me.

"A worthwhile endeavor. Your perspective alone determines the quality of your life, regardless of the circumstances."

"Yes," I say. And I know it down to my bones.

I close the heavy doors of the wardrobe and ask, "But, if I can't see the lenses, how will I know when they are gone?"

"Listen to your heart. The first clue you are viewing life through a false lens is a lack of love in your expression and experience. You may sense a subtle feeling of anxiety or resignation. It is the heart's faint cry that something is out of alignment. When you listen closely to the things you say, the lens gives itself away. When the lie of the lens is exposed, the lens disappears."

"When the lenses disappear, what will I see?"

"You will see and experience truth. You will know you are not alone. You will see there is nothing wrong or that needs to be fixed. Love and connection are always available. You, life, and the world are perfect, just the way you are and just the way you aren't. Your purpose is to follow your bliss."

"I can't imagine!"

"Ah, another lens!" the voice laughs.

19

Something to Wear

I close the wardrobe doors and walk toward the dividing screen and three-panel mirror. In both side panels, I see my reflection. Uncomfortable with the few extra pounds I still carry, I turn away but the silvery reflection in the center panel catches my eye. The hair on my arms rises. I turn back for a second look.

"Ah, the me I forget is not me!" I say.

"Yes."

I gaze at my reflection in the middle panel. My dark hair peeks from under a protective mask. My body is covered with a suit of armor.

"You're right. I can't go home dressed like this."

I lay down my sword and unfasten the strap beneath my chin to remove my battle helmet. The armor clinks and rattles as I unhinge and step out of the metal plated coverings I thought shielded me from hurt but only created a barrier between me and those I love.

"That's curious," I say. "I feel stronger without the armor even though I am defenseless!"

"You are no longer fear's slave."

That's it. I feel *freed*.

I stretch and then shake my head to free the hair that sticks to my neck.

"Much, much better!" I say. "But where are my clothes?"

"Clothes? Ah, yes, of course! Simple, really. At any moment you clothe yourself based on Whether."

"The weather?"

"Whether—whether you choose to be fearful or choose to be confident. Whether you choose to listen to your heart or to the Mountain of Lies. Whether you choose to feel threatened or secure, happy or vengeful. Shackled or free. Your choice of attire is a reflection of your beliefs and intention. It guides your thoughts, your actions, and ultimately the results in your life."

I nod. With choice comes responsibility.

Ah, *Grateful*! You are stunning dressed in *Grateful*!"

I smile. "I choose?"

"You choose."

I step behind the dividing screen. To my surprise, a fourth wardrobe appears, fuzzy at first and then solid. It was not there moments ago.

"When the student is ready, the teacher appears," my thoughts offer above, half in jest, half rationalization.

The wardrobe is tall, majestic. It is topped with a breath-taking pediment of magnificent winged angels that hold an ornate scroll. The scroll reads, "You Choose. Always."

Confused, I ask, "Why was it invisible?"

"You were blind to the law, that you choose, always—even if you let your mood or circumstances do the choosing for you. It is only now that you are intentional with your choice."

Both doors of the wardrobe swing open.

A garment conveyor, like the ones used by dry cleaning shops, whirs and comes to a halt. The abrupt stop causes the clothing on hangers to sway, and then still. I notice the controller on the inside of the cabinet. Two buttons. I push one and watch the garments pass by clockwise. After several minutes without seeing the same garment twice, I realize my possibilities of what to wear are limitless. The garment conveyor belt loops deep into my imagination to present the full range of human possibilities for consideration.

The majority of garments are covered with clear dry cleaner bags. I stop on a section of clothing without the plastic coverings. I flip through the hangers, one at a time, quickly, as if it were a sale rack. *Resigned?* No. *Wary? Weary?* Of course not! *Optimistic? Playful?* Maybe. *Persevering? Cheerful?* Nah. *Judgmental?* Clearly one of my past favorites! *Smart? Motivated? Ambitious?* None of these will do. I pause on *Victim* and laugh out loud. The outfit is striking, expensive, and gorgeous to behold. I've got to look good when I play the role of a victim! *Pathetic* is nothing but rags.

Dedicated, Industrious, Indecisive. No. No. No. Ah, *Nice*. I pull the worn outfit from the hanger and put it on. *Nice* feels comfortable, familiar. I look down and brush the sand off the knees, no doubt from efforts to earn love or approval. I walk to the mirror. My poise and confidence wane. Yuck.

This is not who I am.

"Mountain of Lies! Mountain of Lies!" my thoughts cry in alarm.

I see it! It is the Mountain of Lies at work! *Nice* is my disguise to hide my fear that I will be rejected. Being nice is a strategy to get people to like me or get what I want. *Nice* was my go-to outfit. Not anymore.

"How about *Kind*?" my thoughts ask.

A new outfit appears in the wardrobe. I strip off *Nice* and try on *Kind*.

"That's more like it." My poise and confidence return. The difference between *Nice* and *Kind* becomes clear. When I choose to wear *Nice*, I hope to be rewarded. Not so for *Kind*. Kindness is not a strategy. It is an expression of the real me, void of the influence of the Mountain of Lies. *Kind* hides nothing and wants nothing in return.

Yikes. Most of my well-worn outfits are based on the Mountain of Lies. One truly has to look closely to see. I must choose wisely.

Journey Back to Me

I hang *Kind* on the clothes tree as a possibility and continue to look.

"How about everything in the A's?" I ask aloud. The garment conveyor starts. I watch a myriad of outfits run by for about a half a minute until the conveyor stops. I flip through the outfits. *Accepting, Accomplished, Accountable, Accurate, Adaptive, Adept*. No, no, no. I like the look of *Adventurous*. Next are *Affectionate, Altruistic, Approachable, Assertive*. Nope. I flip through the rest of the A's.

"What about the B's? and C's?"

The conveyor advances. I shuffle through the B's and stop on *Bold*. There are two *Bold* outfits. Curious to know why, I set them both aside. I consider *Caring*. I pass on *Care-free, Celebratory, Challenging, Cheerful, Chivalrous, Committed, Communicative, Compassionate, Compelling, Competent, Competitive, Confrontational, Connected, Conscientious, Considerate, Consistent,* and *Content*. I discover two *Confident* outfits and set both aside. I like *Creative* and *Courageous*.

I collect the two *Bold* and two *Confident* outfits to try on. I put on the first *Bold* and stand in front of the mirror.

"Hmmm."

I take it off and put on the other one. The voice is right! The difference *is* based on Whether, Whether I am bold with the certainty I am worthy and loved or Whether I am bold in spite of the fear I will never be enough! I take the *Bold* outfit based on the Mountain of Lies and toss it to the floor. To my surprise, it does not disappear like my files, grievances, and grudges. My thoughts express my confusion.

The voice hears the commotion and offers an explanation over the partition, "You cannot eliminate a choice. You can only cease to choose to it. Your choice is unlimited. Always."

"Oh."

I pick up *Bold* from the floor and put it back on its hanger. As I go to place it back on its conveyor hook, I spy a pink lump of clothing that must have fallen from its hanger, lying on the bottom of the armoire. As soon as my hand touches the soft fabric, I know I have recovered a treasure.

I squeal with joy and hug the scoop neck t-shirt close to my chest. I give it a vigorous shake and hold it up to the light. It's faded and wrinkled, but it is indeed my shirt, my favorite *stupid* shirt from fifth grade. I giggle as I read its outrageous one-word slogan: *Rockstar*, now barely legible. What fifth-grader doesn't dream of being a rock star? We are all drawn by the mystique of a rebellious boldness that borders on daring, creative magic, and burning desire to express that which is uniquely you. If the shirt wasn't several sizes too small, I would wear it!

"It's too small!" my thoughts cry.

I go to hang up the shirt, and there, right in front of me, hanging on the rack, is a lace-trimmed silk camisole—V-neck, spaghetti straps, the same pink, not faded, with *Rockstar* written across the chest in a dainty soft gray script. My choices truly are unlimited!

I wiggle into the camisole. My secret reminder of who I aspire to be! A rebellious boldness that borders on daring, creative magic, and a passion to bring forth that which is uniquely me can only be a good thing!

"Heart vs. head!" my thoughts cheer.

Heart?

I groan.

"Of course!" my thoughts shout. "I am using my head to choose!"

I ignore the chuckle over the partition.

I can clothe myself with whatever I want to be at any given moment. The choice is mine, always. My choice in attire inspires *everything* I say or do. So, what or who do I want to be? Now? This moment? What inspires *me* most? What expression of myself makes life worth living?

I abandon my alphabetical approach to select my outfit. My heart speaks. I listen.

The garment conveyor whirs and then stops.

I dress.

I return to the three-paneled mirror to admire my attire at every angle. I am awestruck. Instead of armor, I chose to drape myself with the unity of compassion, kindness, humility, gentleness, and patience. My creation. I am clothed in *Love*.

"Ah, the You that you truly are!" says the voice.

"Yes!"

I, too, recognize the serene, capable woman in the reflection. I haven't seen this Liza for so, so long. My bottom lip quivers when my eyes meet hers in the mirror. Silent tears of joy stream down our cheeks.

Then I laugh through the tears.

"I'm sorry! I cry when I am happy too!"

I hear a sniff and turn to see the same tears of joy fall from the eyes.

"So do you! So do you!" I laugh. "Big crybaby!"

We laugh and cry. I spin in circles. My gown of *Love* twirls above my ankles in celebration of the liberation of Liza. I dance with a freedom that would make Mr. Kumar proud.

"It's so beautiful. I am so beautiful! I don't think anyone will recognize me!"

"It's not for them. It's for you, dear Liza."

I am happier than I can remember.

As I go to exit the room I pause in front of the scoreboard. Eyes squint and nose wrinkles as an idea percolates. Before my thoughts can announce my intention, I remove the heavy scoreboard from its anchor and set the bottom of the frame on the floor.

"Just as I thought!" my victorious thoughts sing.

The scoreboard has two sides. On the back, in bold letters the scoreboard reads, "**I**nsults, **I**njuries & **I**njustices to Others."

"*By* Liza," I say.

I am not surprised to see the I's doled out by me far exceed those I received. Michael has the most insults, injuries, and injustices, followed by family, loved ones, and friends.

I hang the scoreboard back in its place with the count of my infractions on display.

"I have much damage to undo!"

The eyes sparkle approval.

"You know what they say about the key to happiness!"

I wait for the answer.

"Cease to count your I's. And toss your G's!"

"Of course!"

I close my eyes as the vault door closes.

20

It's a Practice

When I open my eyes, we are back at the dusty base of rubble from the Mountain of Lies.

"Look! Look!" I shout.

The landscape of my mind is transformed. Fields of pink and white azaleas blossom along the riverbanks. Once anemic, the river's rapid current now bulges against its sturdy banks. The power of the river's current surges in every cell of my body. Billows of my favorite clouds hang weightless in the sky. Coaxed by a gentle breeze, the clouds form a spectacular slow-motion parade against the setting sun. There are fewer molehills in the range to my left. To the far right, beyond the cave, I see a white sand beach and tranquil sea, my new rival for the monstrous roller coaster, now half its original size.

"My landscape! My mind!" I say, with a degree of confidence and power I have not owned in years.

"And, you just started!" says the voice. "Transformation is, after all, just the replacement of a fear-based lie with a newly discovered truth."

Then I see it.

A proud vengeful hill stands in the center where the Mountain of Lies once towered.

"No!" I cry.

"Be prepared, for the Mountain of Lies will sneak back into your thinking and con you of their validity."

I make a vow to myself to stay vigilant. My mind. My life.

"You will catch yourself riding the What-if Roller Coaster and Last-Word Merry-Go-Round. You will find yourself taking a dunk in the Pit of the Past, making mountains out of molehills, collecting grievances, digging holes of sand trying to please others, keeping score of your injustices, and squandering energy on things that do not produce fruit or forward who you truly are."

I nod. I now have a clue what I am up against. My conviction grows.

"Do not punish yourself."

I give a sheepish grin.

"When you discover you have lost your way, simply interrupt the cycle. Get present and stay in the Now. Find a vantage point behind your thoughts so that you can observe them."

"Look but don't touch," I say, remembering how easy it is to let a thought carry me away once I give it the attention it craves.

"Yes."

"Trust yourself and look inside for answers. Never outside. And know without a doubt you are loved beyond measure, dear, dear Liza."

"I will," I promise.

"It takes a lifetime of experiments."

"You mean *experience*."

"Ah! A lifetime of experiments is far more rewarding! If one approaches life as a series of experiments, there is adventure instead of fear of failure. Whether the experiment succeeds or fails, you are victorious! A truth emerges! You are one step closer to understanding what works in life. You learn what's missing and add it. You learn what doesn't belong and take it out. Experimentation is the path to mastery. It leaves no room for the Mountain of Lies. When the experiment fails, you are free to try something new!"

"Instead of taking the failure personally!" I add as another piece of life's puzzle snaps into place. My excitement soars even higher. A powerful way to relate to failure! I will need it.

The river swells, fiercer than ever.

"Yes! It's a practice," says the voice drifting away.

21

Ready or Not

I am back in the white.

"Are you here?" I call out before my thoughts do.

"Always."

And I know that it is true. Only I cut myself off or go away.

I turn around and see the comforting eyes.

"Live, Liza. Create your life. Free from the shackles of fear," urges the voice. "Remember, big problems start with little thoughts."

"And so do dreams come true."

"Yes, dear Liza. Choose well!"

My heart is racing, my palms sweaty. Energy courses throughout my body.

I hesitate.

"I think I am afraid."

"Look inside," says the voice. "What is your relationship to the future? Is it one of dread?"

I look inward. "No," I answer. "I am uncertain of what lies ahead but I look forward to the unfolding of it. There is so much for me to do, even if I am not sure how!"

"That is excitement. It is often confused with fear and can stop us. The physical sensations are the same, but when your relationship to the future is one of anticipation, what you are experiencing is excitement."

"Funny. I always called it panic."

"Funny," the voice retorts, "I didn't see you trying on *Cheeky* back there."

"It's my *Rockstar* camisole," I confess in a whisper. "It's underneath."

"That is so..." looking for the right words, "So, You!"

We laugh.

The tone of the voice turns serious. "Fear may still be present, Liza, but *You* now see it for the fraud that it is."

"Yes," I say.

I swallow hard and look into the eyes. My thoughts are quiet. I see only the reflection of my love mirrored back in the eyes, those beautiful, familiar eyes.

The me that is truly me is going home.

And, I know down to my core, my world and resources are always abundant.

I am more than enough.

I am capable.

I am free.

I am beautiful. And strong.

I am worthy.

I am deserving of love and all good things life has to offer.

I love deeply and am loved back beyond measure.

And I, and only I, am responsible for the choices that create the quality of my life and depth of love in my relationships.

I surrender to the immense wave of gratitude that washes over me. I close my eyes.

"Are You ready?" the voice asks.

"Yes," I say.

And I am.

22

Code 1

B*eep. Beep. Beep.*

What is that noise? It is so annoying! I strain to see the source of the sound. Dizzy pops of light dance around the gray edges of my blurred vision. I feel woozy. Where am I now? Am I back in the gray?

A pair of kind eyes comes into view and then disappears. I calm.

As the gray fades, the stainless safety bars and red-labeled drawers and shelves that line the interior walls of the ambulance come into sharp focus. Mysterious gages, dials, tubing, and cords are mounted or dangle everywhere. On an overhead monitor, green numbers flash as three squiggly lines race in a three-way tie across the screen.

Oh my gosh! I'm back! I'm back!

Wait.

I put my celebration on pause. Why am I in an ambulance? Out of the corner of my eye, I see a bag of clear fluid hanging from the ceiling. The fluid drips into a clear tube that wanders out of my range of vision.

An IV.

Is it mine?

Fear rises.

Somewhere in the recess of my mind, the safety bar of the What-if Worry Coaster locks into place. My fear intends to take me for a joy ride.

I struggle to sit up.

A young woman from behind me steps into view. She is dressed in a navy blue uniform, baby blue disposable medical gloves, and a warm smile. Her long blonde hair is pulled back in a ponytail. Her eyes are kind.

"Don't try to move, Liza. My name is Sherry Dixon. I am a paramedic for the Springville Fire Department. You were in an auto accident. The airbag deployed. You hit your head and were found unconscious. No lacerations though."

Accident? Paramedic? *The coaster car starts up a steep incline.*

"Do you remember the accident?"

The roller coaster car dips downward. An image of the brake lights of the minivan flashes in my mind.

"I hit a white minivan," I say in a shaken voice that does not sound like mine. My clammy body shivers. *The roller coaster car jerks to a half-second halt and begins a second ascent.*

Fearing the worst, I ask, "Was anyone else hurt?"

"The other driver is fine."

Unspeakable relief. I try again to sit up. Why can't I lift my head or move my arms and legs? Panic spreads throughout my body. *The car climbs up, up, up.*

"I can't move!"

"It's ok. Liza. We have you restrained so you can't move your body or turn your head. You are strapped to a backboard and are wearing a neck brace so we can transport you safely and prevent spinal cord injury. It's a precaution until we can take some x-rays and run a few tests." *The car rises higher.*

Sherry steps back to make a call. I try to make out her words. I catch one ominous phrase. Code 1. *The car reaches the top of the peak and teeters.*

Code 1? My mind scrambles to decipher its meaning. What is Code 1?

Sherry completes the call. "Ok! We are on our way to Memorial Hospital. Do you understand?"

The coaster car tips and plunges downwards.

"Yes," I whisper.

Of course, I understand! Code 1! Code 1! My injuries must be really serious! What if I am paralyzed and she doesn't want me to know yet? What if I am never going to walk again? Or, if I have a brain injury! Or worse! Maybe my spine is severed! *The car picks up speed in its downward spiral.*

Sherry sees my fear. She leans over me, stethoscope in hand, looks in my eyes, and asks, "Will you take a deep breath for me, Liza?"

The request snaps me momentarily away from my thoughts.

"Deep breath in. Deep breath out. Just breathe. In and out," she instructs.

My thoughts and breath follow the familiar, comforting words. I focus my attention on a spot on the ceiling of the ambulance. Slowly, I inhale and exhale. The paramedic listens to my lungs. I listen for my heart.

I remember.

There is rare cause for fear in the moment. The danger is almost always *only* in my head. In my thoughts! I get present and watch my worry-filled thoughts. They slow in frequency and intensity. I observe each and let them go. *The worry coaster stops.*

The sign was wrong. There is an exit.

I hop off the roller coaster.

Amazing. From terror to calm in a few breaths! The eyes were right. It *is* a practice! I look newly at my world. Right here, right Now, there is nothing to fear. There is no real danger in this moment. I am safe. It is my choice Whether fear will be my master or I will master my fear. Whether I let circumstance and reaction determine who I am or if I pause to listen for my heart to tell me.

It's my precious life. I want to choose.

Even if I am Code 1.

So, what will it be?

The wardrobe doors open. The garment conveyor whirs deep into my imagination and stops.

I choose *Adventurous*. Why not? There are so many more exciting things to choose than *Scared*!

The outfit slides easily over the secret *Rockstar* camisole I forgot I am wearing.

I retrieve my courage buried deep within and brace myself.

"What is a Code 1?" I ask the paramedic.

"No flashing lights. No siren," Sherry says with a big smile.

I must look confused.

"No siren!" she says with glee. Her baby blue index finger points up.

Her words sink in. The siren of the ambulance is not on. There are no emergency flashing blue lights.

My injuries are considered non-critical! I am not paralyzed! My spinal cord is not severed! A quiet trip to the hospital for x-rays or scans, just to be sure.

I laugh out loud, a combination of deep relief and equal amusement. Oh, the places I let my mind take me! I ignore the paramedic's instructions and try to wiggle my toes. My happy digits obey my command without effort.

I am back!

Alive! And free!

There is so much to do and undo, so much to say and take back and let go. So many wonderful things to practice so I can keep my thoughts and my life free from the influence of the Mountain of Lies.

Will I remember the lessons from my guide and the tour of the landscape of my mind?

Yes.

Always.

Practice! Catch Yourself!

Awareness is the first step to replace destructive thoughts with ones that pull for your happiness and success. Raise your awareness by noticing when destructive thoughts hijack your thinking. Start by journaling in the evening. List the instances you remember. Then up your game through frequent reflection throughout the day.

Collect a Grievance—Instances where you secretly make a mental note of something someone did or said so that you may use it against them in the future.

Collect a Grudge—Instances where you hold something someone did or said (recently or a long time ago) against them and do not forgive them.

Counting Your I's—Instances where you interpret the actions of others to be a personal insult, intentional injury, or injustice and do not forgive them.

Digging Holes in the Sand—Instances where you are doing something or catch yourself doing something in order to be rewarded emotionally in some way by another (appreciation, approval, affection, love).

Growing Fruitless Trees—Instances where your investment of time is fruitless. These are typically activities you use as an escape from tasks you do not want to do or people and circumstances you want to avoid. Areas/activities where you lack passion or you are playing it safe.

Imes and Izzes—Beliefs about yourself, others, or your environment where you have assigned a permanent state to something temporary that you think is true and may not be. *I'm* _____. She, He, or It *is* _____.

In the Punishing Room—Instances where you judge, condemn, chide, or punish yourself for something you did or said or thought (and believe you shouldn't have) or something you did not do or say (and believe you should have).

Last Word Merry-Go-Round—Instances where you mentally rehearse a conversation with another over and over again in your head to either defend yours or someone else's thoughts or actions or attack someone else's thoughts or actions.

Lost in the Pit of the Past—Instances where you find yourself either overcome with regret or longing for the way things were in the past.

Making Mountains out of Molehills—Instances where the insignificant is elevated in importance or where your reaction is incongruent with the event or circumstances. Typically triggered by the need to hide something.

Mountain of Lies—A collection of unquestioned, hidden beliefs that are not true and rob you of power. This includes your shoulds/should nots, must/must nots, and the Ins and Uns (inadequate, insufficient, incapable, indentured, unattractive, unworthy, undeserving)

What-if Worry Coaster—Times where you are worried or concerned about the future, what might happen or what someone else might do, think or say.

If your intention is to lead a
meaningful, joyful, life,
it is best to put practices in place
to help you fulfill that goal.
For additional information on how to
interrupt destructive thinking
and institute new habits
for a more productive and joyful daily experience,
visit:

SheilaDFerguson.com

Reading Guide

For a lively discussion with your book group, consider the following questions:

- How did you experience the book?
- What destructive pattern in thinking did you most relate to and why?
- How did Liza change throughout her tour? Did your opinion of her change?
- What was the most impactful scene or passage?
- Do you agree with the concept of the Mountain of Lies influencing our thinking and ultimately the quality of our lives?
- How different do you think Liza's typical day will be now from the one described in Chapter 1?
- Do you think the fears described in the roller coaster were individual or universal?
- Did the book change your opinion or perspective about anything? Do you feel different now than you did before you read it?
- What lesson did you find the most valuable?
- What was your favorite metaphor used by the author?
- Did the playfulness and humor add or detract from the story?
- Who is the voice/eyes?
- At any point in the book, did you notice your attention shift from the story to a reflection of your own thoughts, life, or relationships? Where did your thoughts take you?
- How did you feel about the ending?

Share your thoughts! Join an online discussion about the book with other readers. Visit *SheilaDFerguson.com* for more details.

Acknowledgements

My warmest admiration and appreciation goes to Lynne Holton. Her illustrations bring playfulness and depth to complement my story. Each rekindles a young curiosity that delights me. Lynne and I made a fine pair. I have never written a book. Lynne has never illustrated one. Together, we put on our *Rockstar* camisoles and embraced the adventure.

Like Liza, I also had a voice to guide me through the journey to write and publish my first story. Since the completion of my first draft, Debbie Justus Kuchta coaxed me along, generously tipping the scales in my favor with her expertise. Thank you, my treasured friend.

A special thank you also goes to Sandy Bohanon, Lori Petrone, Justin Sutherland, Carla Costa, Kay Smith, Lara Scandrett, Kenny Adamcik, and Linda Ruocco. Each left their personal touch in the telling of the story. I am also thankful for the encouragement from Becky Engram, Jane Kendall, Michelle Garcia, Tanya Freach, Janet Fleming, Janet Law, Maureen Dvorak, and fellow writer, Christopher Wang. I will never forget how tenderly he offered feedback, ever so careful not to bruise my writer's spirit, yet unyielding that I deliver nothing less than my best work.

And to Bill, my happily ever after.

About the Author

Sheila Ferguson is a former high tech executive, consultant, and business performance expert. An avid student of personal transformation, Sheila now focuses on her writing. Mother of four boys, now all grown, Sheila lives with her husband in Hilton Head, SC, where she also serves as President of the Women's Association of Hilton Head Island.

Learn more about Sheila at *SheilaDFerguson.com*.

Printed in the United States
By Bookmasters